MW01196670

EASTERN STAR PUBLICATIONS may be ordered with confidence from an old-established and reputable organization. We have been continuously serving the Craft since 1867.

Send for our new list of Eastern Star publications. Prompt attention always given to orders and inquiries.

*****

ORDER
OF THE
EASTERN STAR

An Instructive Manual

On the

ORGANIZATION AND GOVERNMENT

Of

Chapters of the Order

With

RITUAL AND CEREMONIES

———

Arranged by

F. A. BELL

———

(New and Revised Edition)

"To every tie of honor bound,
In love and friendship constant found,
and favored from above."

*"We have seen His star in the East
And have come to worship Him."*

CONTENTS.

NOMENCLATURE AND CLASSIFICATION OF THE GRADES IN FREEMASONRY

SYMBOLIC GRADES

Conferred only in regular Lodges of Master Masons, duly constituted by Grand Lodges

1° Entered Apprentice   2° Fellowcraft
3° Master Mason

INEFFABLE GRADES

4° Secret Master
5° Perfect Master
6° Intimate Secretary
7° Provost and Judge
8° Intendant of the building
9° Master Elect of Nine
10° Master Elect of Fifteen
11° Sublime Master Elected
12° Grand Master Architect
13° Master of the Ninth Arch
14° Grand Elect Mason

Conferred in a Lodge of Perfection, 14°, duly constituted under authority of the Supreme Council of the 33°

ANCIENT HISTORICAL AND TRADITIONAL GRADES

15° Knight of the East or Sword   16° Prince of Jerusalem

Conferred in a Council, Princes of Jerusalem, 16°

APOCALYPTIC AND CHRISTIAN GRADES

17° Knight of the East and West
18° Knight of Rose Croix de H-R-D-M
Conferred in a Chapter of Rose Croix de H-R-D-M, 18°

MODERN HISTORICAL, CHIVALRIC, AND PHILOSOPHICAL GRADES

19° Grand Pontiff
20° Master ad Vitam
21° Patriarch Noachite
22° Prince of Libanus
23° Chief of the Tabernacle
24° Prince of the Tabernacle
25° Knight of the Brazen Serpent
26° Prince of Mercy
27° Commander of the Temple
28° Knight of the Sun
29° Knight of St. Andrew
30° Grand Elect Kadosh or Knight of the White and Black Eagle
31° Grand Inspector Inquistor Commander
32° Sublime Prince of the Royal Secret

Conferred in a Consistory, Sublime Princes of the Royal Secret, 32°.

OFFICIAL GRADES

33° Sovereign Grand Inspector General

Conferred only by the SUPREME COUNCIL, 33°, and upon those who may be elected to receive it by that high body which assembles yearly.

PREFACE.

The spirit of modernity now pervades even our Ancient Mysteries, so that they must bear the stamp of recent investigation. Too little has been written about the splendid Order of the Eastern Star. It is almost impossible to find any printed article bearing on its history, which may be used in making an address on the subject. In this little book will be found a concise account of the development of the Order through the ages, from the early Mysteries to the present time.

An explanation of the purposes of the Order is also included, elucidating the high aims and principles which are responsible for its unprecedented success.

The chapter on Parliamentary Rules of Procedure is also an innovation. It is very difficult to glean the needed facts from the mass of material presented in separate books on Parliamentary Law. In this book is given the information necessary to conduct the business of a Chapter of the Order, and it should prove a welcome addition to the Ritual.

The Ritual itself must remain the same in content: the ceremonies permitting change bear certain improvements in keeping with the trend of the times.

It is believed that a work as noble as that of the Order of the Eastern Star cannot be hindered by the publication of its ceremonies and methods, but that it will rather be furthered by publicity, which is the keynote of this age of Radio and Roentgen Rays.

Therefore in a spirit of reverent appreciation is offered this new and modern Manual of an Order rich in tradition.

F. A. BELL.

THE ORDER OF THE EASTERN STAR

A SHORT HISTORY OF THE ORDER. WITH A BRIEF ACCOUNT OF THE DEVELOPMENT OF SECRET SOCIETIES FOR WOMEN.

Secret societies have always held an attraction for women, as well as for men, in spite of the common belief that women cannot keep a secret. The pages of history show that in past ages women had their own secret societies. In some instances man was excluded as rigorously as woman is excluded from modern Orthodox Freemasonry. In others, men were admitted on equal or almost equal terms with the gentler sex.

The Eleusinian Mysteries were introduced by Eumolpus in 1356 B. C. and were founded in honor of Ceres and Proserpine, and anyone violating the oath taken on admission, or revealing the secrets to the uninitiated was punished with death. The same punishment was meted out to uninitiated intruders at the ceremonies. Into these Mysteries both sexes were eligible for initiation, and there was no age limit.

Then there was the Greek festival of Thesmophoria, held in the month of Pyanepsion (October) in honor of the goddess Demeter. It lasted for five days, and only women were permitted to take part in it. For nine days preceding the Festival they went apart and purified themselves in various ways, in preparation. Participation in the Festival was limited strictly to married women who were full citizens.

Gibbon, in his History of Rome, records a female Order in the fourth century, among the Roman women. No man was ever permitted to be present, or even to be made acquainted with the nature or tendency of the function, and it is impossible to say in what these ceremonies consisted.

Masonry for women, or "Adoptive Lodges" of various kinds, sprung up from time to time. The widow of Charles I of England, daughter of Henry IV, and sister of Louis XIII of France, is said to have been the author of Adoptive Masonry, in the seventeenth century. She is said to have formed a society of women to whom she communicated certain signs and passwords.

In 1712, in Russia, Catherine the Czarina obtained from Peter the Great permission to found the Order of St. Catherine, an Order of Knighthood for women only, of which she was proclaimed Grand Mistress. This was a quasi-Masonic body.

In the eighteenth century there were four Grand Mistresses of the Order of St. John of Jerusalem, which was an emanation of early Masonry.

There is also a story to the effect that Female Freemasonry originated in Holland in 1741, through a woman who secretly witnessed the initiation of her father into the Masonic Order. This is scarcely credited.

In 1771 the Order of Perseverance was established at Paris by several nobles and ladies. It was said to have originated in Poland, but had little of the Masonic character about it.

The real date of the establishment of Adoptive Masonry in France, however, may be placed as 1775, when the Duchess of Bourbon was appointed to the position of Grand Mistress of Adoptive Masonry. Her installation was a very fashionable function, in which about a thousand persons of the elite of French society are said to have assisted.

In 1801 Adoptive Masonry established itself in Holland, where it reigned until June, 1810, when it was peremptorily forbidden.

The Adoptive Rite consisted of four degrees: Apprentice, Companion, Mistress and Perfect Mistress. The first degree was purely symbolical and introductory, intended rather to improve the mind than to convey any definite idea of the institution. The second degree depicted the scene of the temptation in Eden, and the Companion was reminded in a lecture of the penalty incurred by the fall. The third degree alluded to the Tower of Babel and the confusion of tongues as a symbol of a badly regulated lodge, while Jacob's Ladder was introduced as a moral lesson of order and harmony. The fourth degree represented Moses and Aaron and their wives, and the sons of Aaron. The ceremonies referred to the passage of the Red Sea by the Israelites, and the degree was said to symbolize the passage of men from the world of change and discord to a pure land of rest and peace.

The officers of a Lodge of Adoption consisted of Grand Master, Grand Mistress, Orator, Inspector, Inspectress, Depositor, Depositrix, Conductor, and Conductress. The business of each lodge was conducted by the Sisters, the Brethren being looked upon as assistants only. The room was divided into four sections: the west representing Europe; the east, Asia; the south, Africa; and the north, America. Two thrones were erected in the East for the Grand Master and the Grand Mistress, before them was placed an altar, while to their right and left were placed eight statues representing Wisdom, Prudence, Strength, Temperance, Honour, Charity, Justice and Truth. The members sat in two rows, to right and left, at right angles to the two presiding officers: the Brethren armed with swords in the back rows, and the Sisters in the front rows.

The Adoptive Lodges found many opportunities for the practice of benevolence, in which, particularly, they excelled.

The Quadruple Lodge of the Nine Sisters was another prominent Adoptive Lodge, which held several fetes for philanthropic purposes.

Adoptive Masonry was seized by the comprehensive mind of the first Napoleon as a means to consolidate his power, and it rose to favor again on the re-establishment of the Empire. In 1805 the unfortunate Empress Josephine was installed as Grand Mistress of the Imperial Lodge of Adoption of French Chevaliers at Strasbourg when she initiated one of her ladies of honour. It is said that at no period in the history of Adoptive Masonry was there so brilliant a gathering as at this ceremony. It was the first occasion on which French Masonry had been honored with the presence of a sovereign. The ceremonies were most beautiful and impressive.

Adoptive Masonry found its way into Italy, where it flourished as a society for both men and women. By the admission of women into the Order, the terms of the papal denunciation against Freemasons were evaded.

The heads of the Germanic Union countenanced the Order and extended their patronage to the scheme, and at Frankfort the Lodges were composed of persons of rank of both sexes.

The Order of Fendeurs, or Forest Masons, possessed legends claiming a high antiquity. The Fendeurs were, in all probability, a branch of the Carbonari, or Charcoal Burners, a political league which made its appearance in the twelfth century, in Italy. The Lodge room was called a Wood-yard: in summer the meetings were held in a garden. The decorations carried out the effect of a forest, with the various occupations of wood-cutters. The presiding officer was called "Father Master", and the members of both sexes were called "Cousins". Some of the officers were Cousin Hermit, Cousin Wine-dresser, Cousin Bear, Cousin Elm, Cousin Oak. The candidates were called "Briquets".

Various other Lodges succeeded this: The "Order of the Happy People", with nautical emblems and a corresponding vocabulary; the "Companions of Penelope"; the "Dames Phleides"; the "Knights and Nymphs of the Rose"; the "Dames of Mount Tabor", the "Order of Liberty"; "Order of Memphis"; the "Indifferentists" and "The Society of the Chain".

Women were also known in Freemasonry in Egypt, as many as three hundred Greek and Arab women belonging to the Lodges of Alexandria and Cairo alone.

In the United States, also, many societies of the Adoptive Rite were organized, but none were successful until the Order of the Eastern Star was instituted.

The first chapter of the Order of the Eastern Star was organized in Mississippi before the Civil War, but interest flagged until the organization was perfected in 1868. Robert Morris, the inventor of the Order, was a Mason in high standing, and the author of Masonic textbooks of standard authority with the craft. The Order of the Eastern Star is modeled after Freemasonry to a certain extent, and has been called Adoptive Masonry, or the Adoptive Rite. This term is rather mis-leading, however, as the term "Adoptive" implies the power of government and control, and this is not exercised by the Masonic body in regard to the Order of the Eastern Star. Used in connection with this Order, the term means rather a form of ceremonies by which the mothers, wives, daughters and sisters of Freemasons are adopted into Freemasonry. The Masonic Order is strictly a secret society and a Mason may not disclose the mysteries of the order even to members of his family. The Order of the Eastern Star is the result of a desire on the part of the Masons to afford the women of their families as far as possible the benefits and privileges of Freemasonry, and also to secure the help and co-operation of the women in their benevolent projects.

The Order is believed to be the largest Order of women in the world and the fifth largest fraternal organization in existence. Its membership roll is increasing at the rate of fifty thousand a year. Grand Chapters have been organized in various other countries, but the membership is the largest in the United States, numbering about a million and a quarter in 1922.

PURPOSES OF THE ORDER.

The Order of the Eastern Star has several worthy objects: to give the families of Masons social privileges connected with the order; to enlist their sympathy and support for the charitable work of the Masonic body; to help widows and orphans in need, and travellers in distress. It was designed to give certain signs whereby members of the Order of the Eastern Star should make themselves known to Masons and thus secure assistance in emergencies.

The main object of the Order of the Eastern Star is to give practical effect to the beneficent purpose of Freemasonry, particularly in provision for the wives, daughters, widows, mothers and sisters of members of the Craft and at the same time inculcate certain principles. The Order has come to be looked upon as "a strong right arm of Masonry", assisting nobly in its charitable enterprises, helping to secure Masonic Temples, and adding much to the social life of the fraternity. The Adoptive Rite is intended to instill in the members of the Order the deepest realization of the beauties of the moral virtues, the obligations of friendship, and the duties of true womanhood. The various principles emphasized in the Order are five in number, represented by the five Degrees, which are based on five stories from the Bible. They are as follows:

1. Fidelity to vocations of right and duty. This is the teaching of the First Degree, based on the example of Jephthah's Daughter, as set forth in Judges xi. 30-40.

2. Obedience to the demands of honor and justice in all conditions of life. This is the teaching of the Second Degree, as illustrated by the story of Ruth, and is set forth in Ruth 1:16, 17.

3. Loyalty to kindred and friends. This is illustrated in the Third Degree, which is based on the story of Esther and set forth in Esther iv. 2,-vii. 2-5.

4. Trustful faith in the hour of trial. This is the teaching of the Fourth Degree, as illustrated in the life of Martha and set forth in the eleventh Chapter of John.

5. Heroic endurance of the wrongs of persecution when demanded in the defence of truth. This is the teaching of the Fifth Degree, founded on the character of Electa, or

"the elect lady" as shown in the Second Epistle of John.

With this splendid foundation, a wonderful system has been developed, inspiring in its aims and purposes, appealing to the intelligence and moral consciousness as well as to the social instincts of woman-kind. The society also acts as an auxiliary to the Masonic Order, supplementing and aiding in the charitable and benevolent works of the Brethren. The influence of the system is considered to be beneficial in its effects on the Brethren themselves, as a woman's right to adoption into the Order depends upon the affiliation and good standing of the brother through whom she is privileged to join.

When its high aims and purposes are known and understood, then are explained the remarkable growth and success of the Order of the Eastern Star.

GOVERNMENT.

In the Order of the Eastern Star there are three governing bodies; the General Grand Chapter, the Grand Chapter, and the Subordinate Chapter. The General Grand Chapter has the highest rank and has authority, within the limits of the Constitution, over all the other Chapters. Under the General Grand Chapter are the Grand Chapters. A Grand Chapter has jurisdiction over the Order in one State, and paramount authority in all matters except those coming under the control of the General Grand Chapter. The Grand Chapter decides and limits the authority of the Subordinate Chapters within its jurisdiction. Thus there is in the United States one General Grand Chapter. Each state may have one Grand Chapter, and under it, in the towns or neighborhoods are the various Subordinate Chapters. Five Subordinate Chapters may unite to form a Grand Chapter, if there is none in the State.

TO FORM A SUBORDINATE CHAPTER.

To form a Subordinate Chapter of the Order of the Eastern Star seven people who have properly received all of the degrees of the Order petition the General Grand Chapter for a Charter.

The petition must be endorsed by the Master of the nearest Masonic Lodge, or by the Deputy Grand Patron of the Grand Chapter, vouching for the authenticity of the signatures, certifying that each petitioner has received the degrees of the Eastern Star, and stating the relationship of each one to some member of the Masonic order. A Charter will then be issued by the General Grand Chapter. This Charter must always be present at the meetings of the Chapter.

The first board of officers of a new Chapter should be installed by a Grand Matron, or Grand Patron, or a Deputy. At the same time special Inauguration Ceremonies may be held for the new Chapter. These ceremonies will be described in separate chapters of this book.

GENERAL RULES.

Every Chapter has the right to choose and initiate its own members, to elect its officers, and to dispose of its property, with the exception of the charter, record-books, accounts and rituals. These are the property of the General Grand Chapter.

A Subordinate Chapter must make an annual report to the Grand Chapter, of the number initiated, affiliated, withdrawn, suspended, expelled, and deceased. If there is no Grand Chapter in the State, the report shall be made to the General Grand Chapter.

Meetings are Regular or Special. The regular meetings are held at stated times according to the by-laws. Special meetings may be called by the Worthy Matron for the transaction of special business, and only the special business for which it was called may be transacted at a special meeting.

The Charter, and seven members, including one of the first three officers, must be present at a meeting to constitute a quorum.

Meetings of the Chapter must be held in a well guarded room, where the secrets of the order may be preserved. There should be an ante-room adjoining, and also a waiting room for visitors.

An examining committee interviews visitors before the meeting. The visitor must make oath, with the right hand on the Bible, to membership in good standing in a Chapter of the Order of the Eastern Star, with no known reason for being excluded from the meetings of the Chapter.

After the person has given one or more of the signs of the Order, she (or he) may be examined by the customary questions. (The regular form of examination is given and explained by the Worthy Patron in the latter part of the Initiation Ceremonies.)

OFFICERS.

The officers of a Subordinate Chapter are: Worthy Matron, Worthy Patron, Associate Matron, Secretary, Treasurer, Conductress and Associate Conductress, all of whom are elected by separate ballot; and Chaplain, Marshal, Organist, Adah, Ruth, Esther, Martha, Electa, Warder, and Sentinel, who are appointed by the Worthy Matron:

Elections are held annually, and the officers

may be installed at the same meeting, or at the next stated meeting.

The Worthy Matron may at a stated meeting appoint officers to fill the vacancies of appointed officers. Elective officers may be elected to fill vacancies at a stated meeting held for the purpose.

The Associate Matron succeeds the Worthy Matron in case of death, resignation or absence of the Worthy Matron. If both are absent, the Worthy Patron appoints a member to preside until the next annual election.

EAST

W. MATRON.   W. PATRON.

TREAS.   SEC'Y.

NORTH

ASSOCIATE CONDUCTRESS.

FIRST CONDUCTRESS.

SOUTH

ASSOCIATE MATRON.

WARDER.

(ROOM FOR PREPARATIONS
EXAMINATIONS, ETC.)

SENTINEL.
(ANTE ROOM)

WEST

STATIONS OF THE OFFICERS.

The permanent stations of the officers in the Lodge Room are as follows: In the East: Worthy Matron and Worthy Patron. In the Northeast, Treasurer. In the Southeast, Secretary. The Chaplain is stationed a little in front and to the right of the Treasurer, and the Marshal in front and to the right of the Secretary. In the West, the Associate Matron. In the Southwest, the Warder. The Sentinel occupies a position just outside the door on the Southwest. In the South, Conductress. In the North, Associate Conductress.

In the center of the floor of the room is a large five-pointed star with an altar in the center, on the altar an open Bible. Each point of the star is painted with one of the five colors of the order; th white point toward the West. Adah is stationed on the blue point, Ruth on the yellow point, Esther on the white point, Martha on the green point, and Electa on the red point. Their chairs may either face the East, or be turned slightly toward the altar. The side of the room where the presiding officer sits at the dais is called "The East."

FURNITURE AND REGALIA.

There should be a pedestal with gavel, in the East, for the use of the presiding officer. One blow of the gavel calls the meeting to order, is a signal to be seated, and also completes the closing of the meeting. The officers rise at two blows from the gavel, and at three blows the entire Chapter rises.   •   • •   • • •

There are special Badges for each officer, and these must be worn during the chapter meetings. Each officer has a special jewel of gold or gilt, suspended from a ribbon having the five colors of the order. These colors are: blue for Jepthah's daughter, yellow for Ruth, white for Esther, green for Martha, and Red for Electa. The General Grand Chapter also prescribes collars, robes and other regalia which may be worn if desired. The regular regalia of the order is a scarf of the five colors, three inches wide, with a rosette on the shoulder, breast, and at the crossing. It is worn from the right shoulder to the left side.

There are various banners for the Order, which may be displayed at the meetings. These banners are about twelve by eighteen inches, and are colored and inscribed as follows: Love (white), Peace (blue), Faith (green), Charity (white), Hope (green), Truth (red), Virtue (blue), Wisdom (red).

There should be in each Chapter room some Bibles, a Seal, the Signet of the Order, a sword and veil for Adah; sheaf and culms of artificial barley for Ruth, Esther's crown and scepter, a broken column for Martha, and a cup for Electa.

JEWELS AND BADGES.

The jewels for the various officers are as follows:

For the Worthy Matron—Five-pointed Star, with Gavel in center.

For the Worthy Patron—Five-pointed Star. with Square and Compass in center.

For the Associate Matron — Five-pointed Star, with full Sun in center.

For the Secretary—Five-pointed Star, with Cross-pens in center.

For the Treasurer—Five-pointed Star, with Cross-keys in center.

For the Conductress — Five-pointed Star, with crossed Scroll and Baton in center.

For the Associate Conductress—Five-pointed Star, with Baton in center.

For the Chaplain—Five-pointed Star, with Bible in center.

For the Marshal—Five-pointed Star, with Batons crossed in center.

For the Organist—Five-pointed Star, with Lyre in center.

For Adah—Triangle, with Sword and Veil in center.

For Ruth—Triangle, with Sheaf in center.

For Esther — Triangle, with Crown and Scepter in center.

For Martha—Triangle, with Broken Column in center.

For Electa—Triangle, with Cup in center.

For Warder—Five-pointed Star. with Dove in center.

For Sentinel — Five-pointed Star. with Crossed Swords in center.

Each of the above jewels, enclosed in a Pentagon, is suitable for the Grand Chapters; these in turn, within a circle, are the appropriate jewels for the General Grand Chapter.

The Worthy Matron is also entitled to wear a special scarf, in addition to her Jewel. It is worn from the left shoulder to the right side, and is made of purple velvet. It is three inches wide, and is edged with gold lace on the inner edge, and gold fringe on the outer edge. Upon the shoulder is a five-pointed star embroidered in silk in the five colors of the Order. At the crossing is a gold rosette with two gold tassels hanging from it.

There is a regular membership badge which may be worn during the meetings of the Chapter. This may worn on the left breast by any

JEWELS OF OFFICERS

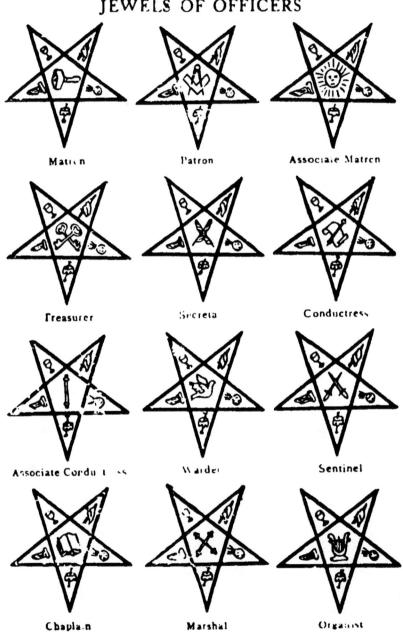

Matron　　　　　Patron　　　　Associate Matron

Treasurer　　　　Secreta　　　　Conductress

Associate Condu t ss　　Warder　　　　Sentinel

Chaplain　　　　Marshal　　　　Organist

JEWELS OF OFFICERS

Adah

Ruth

Esther

Martha

Electa

member attending the meeting. It has a five-pointed star, and the five colors of the order.

Special attention should be given to the use of flowers; to the lighting arrangement, and to the music, for they add much to the beauty and impressiveness of the ceremonies when skillfully adapted to the meaning of the Rites.

THE LANDMARKS OF THE ORDER.

There are certain elementary principles upon which the whole system of the order is erected. Whatever is essential to the existence of the Order of the Eastern Star as an organized institution is one of these elementary principles. They are axiomatic and fundamental, and are properly called Landmarks, because they are the bounds set up to mark out and distinguish the Order of the Eastern Star from every other organization. Should these be removed the Order would lose its efficiency, even its very life, and cease to exist. For the life of the Order is its principles, together with its peculiar method of teaching and enforcing them upon the hearts of the members. A brief statement of these principles follows:

1. The name of the Order is unchangeable.

2. There are five degrees of the Adoptive Rite which shall be permanent in name and in character.

3. The means of recognition are unchangeable.

4. The Order is founded upon a belief in a Supreme Being.

5. The lessons of the Rite are taken from the Scriptures, the teachings are moral, and the expressed purposes are beneficent.

6. The binding force of the vows of the order, voluntarily · assumed, is perpetual. There is no release from its obligations.

7. These obligations are founded on the honor of the individual members who have obtained its secrets. They are framed upon the principle that whatever benefits are due from the Masonic Brotherhood to the wives, mothers, daughters, widows and sisters of Masons, similar good offices are also due from them to the Fraternity.

8. The Subordinate Chapter may enforce the laws of the Order, to which every member is subject.

9. An offending member may be tried by the Chapter to which the member belongs, or by the Chapter within whose jurisdiction the member resides.

10. The Grand Chapter has authority over the Subordinate Chapter, and any member may appeal to the Grand Chapter or its head for a decision over-ruling the decision of the Subordinate Chapter.

11. Every member has the right to visit

any regular Chapter, unless this is lawfully opposed by members of that Chapter.

12. Each Chapter has the right to decide upon its own membership, choosing from the eligible candidates.

13. Candidates for the degrees, or membership, are elected by secret ballot, which must be unanimous and without debate.

14. A Brother in good standing shall preside over the initiation ceremonies. The degrees cannot be conferred unless this rule is observed, although the Worthy Matron may assist.

TO OPEN THE CHAPTER.

Before the opening exercises the officers, except the Worthy Patron and Associate Conductress retire to the ante-room. The Worthy Patron ascends the dais in the East, and gives one blow with the gavel, to call the meeting to order. He requests those who are not members to leave the room, and then instructs the Associate Conductress to bring in the officers. As they enter, the Chapter stands, called up by three gavel blows. Music may be played while the officers march in, in two files, as follows, led by the Conductress and Associate Conductress:

Associate Conductress	Conductress
Treasurer	Secretary
Chaplain	Marshal
Electa	Adah
Martha	Ruth
Esther	Warder
Associate Matron	Worthy Matron

The Worthy Matron and Associate Matron step toward the center. The Worthy Patron then instructs the Conductress to escort the Worthy Matron to the East. Music may be played at this time. The Worthy Matron receives the gavel and assumes charge of the meeting.

W. M. The officers will take their regular stations and prepare for the work of the Chapter.

[With one blow of the gavel, the Worthy Matron seats the Chapter. A chord may be played for the rising and seating of the Chapter. When the Worthy Matron calls on an officer, the officer rises, saying "Worthy Matron", and remains standing during the remainder of the opening ceremonies.]

W. M. Sister Warder, will you see that all doors are securely closed.

War. They are secure, Worthy Matron.

W. M. Sisters, Brothers, and Visitors of .... Chapter, No. ...... of the Order of the Eastern Star, the time has come for us to resume our activities. To open our Chapter in a manner appropriate to our work, and to insure the best results, I solicit your careful attention and assistance. Sister Associate Matron, you will make sure that all present are members of this order.

[If the Associate Matron is able to vouch for all present, she does so. If not, she says:]

A. M. Sister Conductress, and Sister Associate Conductress, ascertain and report whether all present are entitled to be here.

[These two officers pass through the room from the East to the West, one on each side of the room, questioning those with whom they are not acquainted. They use the customary means of examination, as given in a previous chapter of this book. (Soft music should be played at this time.) Only those who have received all five degrees of the Order are permitted to be present at the opening ceremonies.

The Conductresses resume their stations, and the Associate Conductress makes her report to the Conductress, who says:]

Cond. Sister Associate Matron, all present are members of the Order, and are entitled to be here.

A. M. Worthy Matron, all present are entitled to be here, being members of the Order of the Eastern Star.

W. M. Very well. Sister Warder, you will instruct the Sentinel that we are occupied with the opening ceremonies of our Chapter, and direct him to permit no interruption.

[Whenever the Warder communicates with the Sentinel, she raps five times on the door, thus: - - -- —. The Sentinel answers by repeating these raps in the same way. Then the Warder knocks once and the Sentinel answers with one knock. The Warder then opens the door, instructs the Sentinel, closes the door and says:]

War. Worthy Matron, there will be no disturbance or interruption from the outside.

[The Worthy Matron, with two gavel blows, calls the officers to arise, and they remain standing during the opening ceremonies.]

W. M. Sister Associate Matron, what number of officers is required to constitute a Chapter of this Order, and what are their titles?

A. M. Worthy Matron, a complete Chapter of the order requires seventeen officers. Their titles are: Worthy Matron, Worthy Patron, Associate Matron, Secretary, Treasurer, Conductress, Associate Conductress, Chaplain, Marshal, Organist, Adah, Ruth, Esther, Martha, Electa, Warder, and Sentinel.

W. M. Where is the Sentinel stationed?

A. M. The Sentinel is stationed outside the closed door, Worthy Matron.

W. M. Give an explanation of his duties and of his badge of office.

A. M. His duty is to protect the Chapter against the intrusion of unqualified persons. His badge of office is the Cross-swords within the star, and is an emblem of protection. It reminds him that our security from interruption during the solemn services of the order is dependent upon his watchful care.

[It is not necessary to have the duties and badges of the officers explained at each meeting. That part of the ceremony may be omitted when desired, although it must not be left out of the Ritual permanently.]

W. M. Locate the Warder's station.

A. M. The Warder's station is at the Southwest entrance to the Chapter room, Worthy Matron.

W. M. Sister Warder, give an explanation of your duties and your badge of office.

War. To act in association with the Sentinel to prevent intrusions and interruptions. My badge of office is the Dove within the Star, an emblem of peace, reminding me that peace and harmony are essential to the work of our Order, and that it is my duty to promote them.

W. M. Locate the station of the Associate Conductress.

War. The Associate Conductress is stationed in the North, Worthy Matron.

W. M. Sister Associate Conductress, give an explanation of your duties and your badge of office.

A. C. Worthy Matron, my duties are to receive and prepare candidates for initiation, and to assist the Conductress. My badge is the Baton within the Star. It is an emblem of direction, reminding me that good discipline must be maintained for the success of the order.

W. M. Locate the station of the Conductress.

A. C. The Conductress is stationed in the South, Worthy Matron.

W. M. Sister Conductress, explain your duty and your badge of office.

Cond. To obey your instructions, Worthy Matron; to assist the Associate Matron, and to conduct the candidates through the initiation ceremonies. My badge is the Scroll and Baton within the star. It is an emblem of prepared plans and their accomplishment. It reminds me that I must execute my duties worthily, giving the candidate a good and lasting impression as she is conducted through the labyrinth of our rite.

W. M. Locate the station of our Secretary.

Cond. Our Secretary is stationed in the Southeast, Worthy Matron.

W. M. Sister Secretary, explain your duties and your badge of office.

Sec. Worthy Matron, my duties are to keep

a record of the proceedings of the Chapter; to conduct its correspondence; to receive all money for the Chapter, turning it over to the Treasurer, and taking her receipt for it. My badge is the Cross-pens within the Star, an emblem of intelligence. It reminds me to be loyal to my obligations, careful that the money entrusted to me shall be handled according to the rules of the Chapter, and that the good deeds of my associates in the Order may not go unrecorded.

W. M. Locate the station of the Treasurer.

Sec. The Treasurer is stationed in the Northeast, Worthy Matron.

W. M. Sister Treasurer, explain your duties and your badge of office.

Treas. Worthy Matron, my duty is to receive all money from the Secretary, giving her my receipt, and paying it out only upon the proper authority. My badge is the Cross-keys within the Star, an emblem of security, reminding me that I must be faithful to my trust, in order that the Chapter may meet its expenses and carry on its charitable work of relief to the distressed.

W. M. Locate Adah's station.

Treas. Adah is stationed at the first, or

blue point of the Star, Worthy Matron.

W. M. Sister Adah, explain your duty and the significance of your special color and emblem.

Adah. Worthy Matron, my duty is to reveal to all proper inquirers the light, knowledge and beauty of the Blue ray, which represents a cloudless sky, and symbolizes faithfulness. My badge is the Sword and Veil within the Triangle, symbolizing the heroic conduct of Jephthah's Daughter, whom I personate in our Rite.

W. M. Give the sign of Adah, and explain it.

Adah. A lady having a veil on, in the usual manner, first pulls it down over her face, then three times in succession raises it, by taking one corner with the right and the other with the left hand, and when lifting it the third time throws the veil over the top of her head, and holding onto the corner looks up. This is called the "Daughter's Sign".

A Brother or Sister seeing this sign, answers, "Alas, my daughter!" which is the pass. The sign alludes to the refusal of Jephthah's Daughter to have her face covered when about to be executed. The pass is used to recall the lamentable but glorious event to which the entire history of Jephthah's Daughter refers.

W. M. Locate Ruth's station.

Adah. Ruth is stationed at the second or Yellow point of the Star, Worthy Matron.

W. M. Sister Ruth, explain to us your duties, and the significance of your especial color and emblems.

Ruth. Worthy Matron, my duty is to reveal to all proper inquirers the light, knowledge and beauty of the Yellow ray, whose golden lustre symbolizes constancy. My badge is the Sheaf within the Triangle. It is a symbol of plenty, and represents the reward of diligence, as exemplified by Ruth, the patient and humble gleaner whom I personate in our Rite.

W. M. Give the sign of Ruth, and explain it.

Ruth. Take handfuls of barley heads in each hand, or use something to represent culms of barley, filling the hands and sticking out a few inches. Then extend the hands in front as if to display their contents, and next cross the wrists on the breast, the contents of each hand pointing upward toward the shoulders, also looking upward. The sign alludes to Ruth holding out two handfuls of barley to Boaz, and appealing mutely to God. A Sister or Brother seeing this sign, answers, "Who is this?" which is the pass of this degree. The pass is used to recall the then lowering but afterwards glorious history of the heroic Ruth.

W. M. Locate the station of Esther.

Ruth. Esther is stationed at the third, or White point of the Star, Worthy Matron.

W. M. Sister Esther, explain to us your duties, and the significance of your especial color and emblem.

Esther. Worthy Matron, my duty is to reveal to all proper inquirers the light, knowledge and beauty of the White ray, which is a symbol of light, purity and joy. My badge, the Crown and Scepter together within the Triangle, is symbolic of royalty and power. In exercising authority, we should ourselves be ruled by justice and unselfish devotion to the welfare of others. Esther, whom I personate in this Rite, saved her people from destruction by the practice of these principles.

OPENING CEREMONIES.

W. M. Give the sign of Esther, and explain it.

Esther. The sign of Esther is made by three motions. Raise the right hand, the palm downward, a little over the head as if touching a crown there. Throw the hand forward, as if touching a scepter held by the opposite person, the hand on a level with the eyes. Carry the hand to the left breast.

The sign alludes to the manner of Queen Esther's appearance before King Ahasuerus, as explained in the history of the degree. Brothers and Sisters, on seeing this sign given, should answer ''What wilt thou?'' which is the pass of this degree. The pass is used to recall the grand sacrifice and triumphant success of the heroic Esther.

W. M. Locate the station of Martha.

Esther. Martha is stationed at the fourth or Green point of the Star, Worthy Matron.

W. M. Sister Martha, explain to us your duties and the significance of your especial color and emblem.

Martha. Worthy Matron, my duty is to reveal to all proper inquirers the light, knowledge and beauty of the Green ray, which is symbolic of nature's loveliness, and is an emblem of Hope and Immortality. My badge, the Broken Column within the Triangle is emblematic of the death of one cut off in the strength and vigor of life. It recalls the sisterly grief of Martha, whom I personate in our Rite.

W. M. Give the sign of Martha and explain it.

Martha. Join the hands together at the tips of the thumbs and fingers, forming the figure of a triangle. Raise the triangle thus formed directly above the eyes. Raise the eyes, looking through the triangle. A Brother or Sister, seeing this sign, answers "Believest thou this?" which is the pass of this degree. The pass will recall the spirit of fidelity which characterizes the history of Martha. The sign refers to Martha's trustful appeal.

W. M. Locate the station of Electa.

Martha. Electa is stationed at the fifth or Red point of the Star, Worthy Matron.

W. M. Sister Electa, explain to us your duty and the significance of your especial color and emblem.

Electa. Worthy Matron, my duty is to reveal to all proper inquirers the light, knowledge and beauty of the Red ray, which symbolizes the fervor which should impel all who are devoted to the service of truth. My badge is the Cup within the Triangle, which is emblematic of charity and hospitality. It com forts us by reminding us that although our cup of sorrow may seem to be overflowing, it will finally be filled with rich and heavenly blessings, "good measure, pressed down and running over."

W. M. Give the sign of Electa and explain it.

Electa. Cross the hands on the breast as if clasping something to the bosom, at the same time looking up. The sign alludes to Electa's clasping the crucifix to her bosom, representing her love for the Saviour. A Brother or Sister, seeing this sign, answers, "Love one another," which is the pass of this degree. It is used to recall the summing up of the grand tragedy which crowned the life of the heroic Electa.

W. M. Very good. When we are hailed by a member of the Order with any one of these signs, let us each recall the virtues of the character whose sign is given, and give an attentive answer.

W. M. Sister Electa, locate the station of the Associate Matron.

Electa. The Associate Matron is stationed in the West, Worthy Matron.

W. M. Sister Associate Matron, explain your duties and your badge of office.

A. M. Worthy Matron, my duty is to assist the Worthy Matron in her work in the Chapter, and to preside when she is absent from a meeting. My badge is an emblem of light, the radiant Sun within the Star, reminding me that so should the splendid principles of the Order of the Eastern Star shine unceasingly through our lives.

W. M. Locate the station of the Worthy Patron.

A. M. The Worthy Patron is stationed at your left, Worthy Matron.

W. M. Explain the duties of the Worthy Patron and his badge of office.

A. M. The Worthy Patron acts as a general supervisor over the Chapter. He advises the Worthy Matron, oversees the work of the other officers, presides over the meeting when the degrees are conferred, and at any other time when requested to do so by the Worthy Matron. His badge of office is the Square and Compass within the Star, emphasizing the connection between the Masonic Fraternity and the Order of the Eastern Star.

W. M. Locate the station of the Worthy Matron.

A. M. The Worthy Matron is stationed in the East, Worthy Matron.

W. M. Explain her duties and her badge of office.

A. M. The Worthy Matron is the acting head of the Chapter. She maintains obedience to the rules of the Order; presides over the meetings, and regulates the business of the Chapter. Her badge is the Gavel within the Star, significant of her authority. It counsels her to prayerful realization of her responsibilities to God, to loyal devotion to her duties and to the Chapter whose success depends upon her judgment and discretion exercised in the spirit of faith and prayer.

W. M. In this spirit I desire to open our Chapter and to perform the duties which may devolve upon me. Let us unite in prayer for the needed grace to do our work well.

[The Worthy Matron calls up the Chapter by

two gavel blows. The Chaplain or the Worthy Patron offers prayer from the Altar.]

PRAYER.

Oh Lord, the Giver of all blessings, look upon us in our humble efforts to promote truth, and love and peace in this beautiful world of Thy creation. Embue us with divine love, which shall overcome all enmity and discord. Give us the grace of charity for all, making us tender hearted, forgiving one another. Fill our hearts with the desire to serve thee with good works, believing that our honest labors will reap their reward. Bless and prosper the work of our Chapter and grant that finally we may all enjoy those blessings which Thou has promised to them that love three. Amen.

Prayers are followed by the response from the members, "So may it be."

W. M. Let us sing together an Opening Ode.

OPENING ODE.

Air—"Just Before the Battle, Mother."

Here around the altar meeting,
    Where the sons of light combine;
Mingled with our friendly greeting,
    Is the glow of love divine;

For this Hall to virtue given,
    And our emblems on the wall,
Point us to the Lodge in Heaven,
    And the Master of us all

Chorus—Keep in view the Lodge supernal,
    Life is love enthroned in heaven,
Where the true light never wavers,
    And our mortal sins forgiven.

In the bonds of Mason's duty,
    Seek we now the Mason's light,
Forms of Wisdom, Strength and Beauty
    Teach us what is good and right;
Far be every sinful passion,
    Near be every gentle grace;
And so at last this holy mission
    Shall reveal our Master's face.

Chorus—Keep in view the Lodge supernal, etc.

OPENING CEREMONIES.

W. M. Sister Conductress, attend at the Altar.

[The Conductress opens the Bible on the Altar.]

W. M. Sisters and Brethren, I do now declare .... Chapter, No. ......, Order of the Eastern Star, open for the business of the Chapter. Sister Warder, you will so inform the Sentinel.

[The Warder, after the regular raps (— — — — — —) duly answered by the Sentinel, closes the door and reports:]

War. Your instructions have been obeyed, Worthy Matron.

[The Worthy Matron seats the Chapter with one gavel blow, and the business of the meeting is transacted.

As soon as the business of the meeting is finished the Worthy Matron resumes as follows:]

W. M. Sister Associate Matron, is there any further business to come before this meeting?

A. M. Worthy Matron, I know of no further business.

W. M. Sister Warder, you will instruct the Sentinel to allw no interruption while we are closing the Chapter.

[The Warder instructs the Sentinel — — — — — —.]

War. Worthy Matron, your instructions have been obeyed.

W. M. It is well. Let us all join in singing a closing ode.

[She calls the Chapter up, and all sing the Closing Ode.]

W. M. Let us pray.

[The Chaplain or Worthy Patron makes the prayer at the Altar, as at the opening exercises.]

CLOSING PRAYER.

Our Father, merciful and holy, who hearest and answerest the humble petitions of Thy children, let Thy spirit of love descend upon us. Make us ever mindful of our duties to mankind and to Thee. Permit us to meet here again in truth and in love, with honor to Thee, that we may advance in wisdom and in service to our fellow men. In Thy name do we pray. Amen.

Members. So may it be.

[After prayer, the Chaplain (or Worthy Patrons) takes a place in the circle of officers and faces the East.]

W. M. Sister Conductress, minister at the Altar.

[The Conductress closes the Bible, and steps back into the officers' circle, facing the East.]

W. M. Sisters and Brethren, we fare forth into the life of the world, unaware of the trials which may be ahead of us. Let us not be afraid, for we have tne promise of our heavenly Father that He will strengthen us and support us by His might and power Farewell.

Members. Farewell.

W. M. This meeting of .... Chapter, No. .... is now closed. Sister Warder, you will please instruct the Sentinel.

[The Worthy Matron closes the meeting with one blow of the gravel.

The Warder notifies the Sentinel that the Chapter is closed.]

THE INITIATION.

The Candidates for initiation, having been notified by the Secretary of their election to membership, assemble in the ante-room at the time of a regular meeting. Both men and women may receive the degree at the same initiation, and the words of the initiation ceremony must be changed to suit the case. At least nine officers are needed to confer the degrees, including the Worthy Patron, or a Mason acting for him.

W. M. Sister Conductress, you will ascertain whether there are in waiting any candidates for the degrees.

[The Warder gives the usual raps — — — — — — and opens the door on receiving the response from the Sentinel. The Associate Conductress goes out into the ante-room, learns the names of the Candidates, and then returns to the Chapter room.]

A. C. Worthy Matron, I find .... waiting to receive the degrees.

W. M. (Offering the gavel) Worthy Patron, the Associate Conductress reports that there is a candidate waiting to receive the degrees of our Order. Will you preside over the meeting during the conferring of the degrees?

W. P. Sister Secretary, has this petitioner been duly elected to receive the degrees of the Order?

Sec. Yes, Worthy Patron.

W. P. Sister Associate Conductress, you will retire to the preparation room and make ready the candidate.

[She retires, proceeding as before, and says to the candidate:]

A. C. Do you believe in a Divine Being, who is God of the Universe?

Cand. Yes, I do.

A. C. Friend, this life is a labyrinth through which we all roam blindly and, alas, all too frequently in ignorance. It is well to learn from the experience of others, profiting by their wisdom and example. Those whom experience has taught may impart their knowledge to the unenlightened. Allow me therefore, as one who knows the intricate mazes of our Rite, to act as your counsellor at this time, preparing you for the ceremonies of initiation.

[Following this speech the Associate Conductress proceeds in the preparation of the candidate, removing her hat, gloves and wrap. She then throws a thin white veil over the head and face of the candidate and conducts her to the door leading into the Chapter room. **The Associate** Conductress gives the usual raps — — — — —.]

Cond. Worthy Patron, I hear an alarm at the door of the preparation room.

W. P. Sister Conductress, ascertain for us the cause of this alarm.

[The Conductress goes to the door and gives the answering raps — — — — —, and opens the door.]

Cond. Who knocks at the door of our Chapter room?

A. C. The Associate Conductress with a candidate who seeks initiation into our Order.

Cond. Has she been properly prepared?

A. C. She has.

Cond. Wait, my friend, for orders from the Worthy Patron.

[The Conductress closes the door, **faces the** Worthy Patron and says:]

Cond. Worthy Patron. the alarm was **given** by the Associate Conductress who is accompanied by a candidate waiting to receive the degrees of the Order.

W. P. Has the candidate been properly prepared for initiation?

Cond. She has.

W. P. You may admit her.

[The lights may be lowered and soft music played during the entrance of the candidate and the following speech of the Conductress. The Conductress opens the door and leads the candidate into the room.]

Cond. Doubtless you have well considered the step you are now taking in entering this Order, which is dedicated to the principles of Charity, Truth and Loving Kindness. By your own free choice you are here. Complain not, therefore of any trials. Upon your lips is set a seal. Be warned thereby to preserve eternal silence and secrecy concerning those things which may be revealed to you here. Be not weary in well-doing. Woe unto those who seek to take upon themselves burdens which they are unable to bear. Woe unto the faithless and insincere who assume obligations lightly and straightway forget them. "Trust in the Lord with all thine heart and lean not to thine own understanding. In all thy ways acknowledge Him and He will direct thy paths."

[While the music continues (or, lacking music, the Worthy Patron recites from 1st Cor., 15th Chap.), the candidate, leaning on the right arm of the Conductress, is led all around the room. If

there is more than one candidate the Associate
Conductress also assists. Coming up to the Associate Matron, the Conductress says:]

Cond. Sister Associate Matron I take
pleasure in introducing to you ....
whom you will present to the Worthy Matron.

[Each officer arises as the Conductress intro-
duces the Candidate, and remains standing until
they have passed on to the next point of instruction.]

A. M. My friend, you are truly welcome.
Sister Conductress, will you have the candidate to face the East........ Worthy Matron,
allow me the honor of presenting ....
whose petition has been approved by this
Chapter, and who is now prepared to accept
the obligation of our Order.

W. M. I welcome you into this Chapter
with pleasure. Your connection with the
Masonic Order, and the recommendations
which you bring, assure us that you are
worthy to be entrusted with the light and
knowledge of our Order. One of the beneficent
purposes of Freemasonry is to secure the
welfare of the mothers, wives, sisters and
daughters of Master Masons. The Order of
the Eastern Star is designed to further this
aim. The Masonic principles of Fraternal

Love, Friendly Aid, and Truth are here declared and taught. As we journey through life's labyrinthian mazes we unite for cheerful companionship and pleasant society, nor do we fail to extend comfort, aid and protection, one to the other.

We have in our Order certain secrets which enable us to recognize each other at any time. These secrets will be divulged to you in due time.

There is a Grand Chapter of the Order of the Eastern Star which formulates the laws and regulations governing the Subordinate Chapters, of which this is one. We have framed our own By-laws. These laws, regulations and by-laws each member of the Order is bound to obey. We shall expect you to share in this obedience.

W. M. Worthy Patron, I take pleasure in introducing to you this candidate, who is ready and willing to undertake the obligations or our Rite.

W. P. Our obligation is a solemn pledge which you must make before you may enjoy the privileges of our Order. It binds you to strict secrecy concerning the work of the Order, and to the performance of those deeds of charity and mercy upon which depends the success of the Order of the Eastern Star. If you are willing to assume the obligation, we will proceed. Are you willing?

Cand. Yes, Worthy Patron.

W. P. Sister Conductress, you will lead the candidate to the Altar to receive the obligation.

[The candidate is led to the Altar while music is played or sung. While she kneels, facing the East, a Bible is placed in her hands. She holds it open against her breast, fingers interlaced over the book, thumbs holding the edges against her breast. The music continues softly. The Worthy Patron calls the Chapter to rise (by three gavel blows), and he himself takes his position at the East of the Altar. He gives the Obligation, which is repeated by the candidate.]

OBLIGATION.

I hereby pledge the sacred honor of a woman (or a Master Mason) to the faithful performance of the conditions of the following obligation: I will maintain with vigilance the absolute secrecy to which I now assent, promising never to reveal unlawfully any of the ceremonies, signs or passes of the Order of the Eastern Star.

I will not be present nor assist in conferring these degrees on any man not Masonically known by me to be a Master Mason, nor any lady not vouched for by a Master Mason as being the wife, widow, sister, mother or daughter of a Master Mason.

I will obey the constitution and laws and regulations of the Grand Chapter, and the by-laws of the Subordinate Chapter of which I may be a member.

I will relieve the necessities of a brother or sister of these degrees, (if they apply to me as such and are found worthy), as far as their necessities may require and my ability permit.

Furthermore, I will not speak disrespectfully of a worthy brother or sister of these degrees, but will give them due and timely notice, that they may ward off approaching danger.

In the presence of Almighty God, and before these witnesses, I do make this solemn pledge.

[The Conductress takes the Bible from the Candidate.]

W. P. (extending his hand) Arise, Sister ...., your pledge is accepted and we

share with you in our Covenant of Adoption.
You will now be made a member of our Order,
and conducted through its labyrinth, to the
several points of the Star, receiving instruction
along your journey regarding those virtuous
characters whom we seek to emulate.

[The lights are turned on, the Worthy Patron
returns to the dais in the East, and seats the
Chapter. The Conductress leads the candidate all
around the Star, and up to the first point, facing
Adah. Music should be played, or in the absence
of music, the Worthy Patron recites Proverbs 3;
13, 15, 17. The Conductress removes the veil of
the candidate.]

Cond. Sister Adah, I bring to you this sister, who, pledged to our Obligation and sharing in our Covenant of Adoption, will receive
instructions from you on the sanctity of a
vow, and faithfulness to convictions of right,
as forcibly delineated in the Book of Judges
in the history of Jephthah's Daughter.

Adah. The history of Jephthah's Daughter,
as composing a degree of the Order of the
Eastern Star, is thus given:

Her father, Jephthah, was the ninth judge
of Israel. He was a resident of Mizpeh, in
the mountains of Gilead, a warrior, and a man
of decided personal character.

Being called upon, in the extremity of his country's trials, to go at the head of its armies and resist the Ammonites, its enemies, he prepared his household for a campaign that would perhaps cost him his life, and then committed himself to the protection of God in solemn prayer. It was an age when religious knowledge was scanty, and man knew but little of his Maker's will. Jephthah thought to propitiate Deity by a vow, such as his forefathers had made when about to depart upon dangerous enterprises. And this is the record of his vow, as found in the 11th chapter of the Book of Judges:

"Jephthah uttered all his words before the Lord in Mizpeh.

"And Jephthah vowed a vow unto the Lord, and said, If thou shalt without fail deliver the children of Ammon into mine hands,

"Then it shall be that whatsoever cometh forth of the doors of my house to meet me, when I return in peace from the children of Ammon, shall surely be the Lord's, and I will offer it up for a burnt-offering."

The victory was gained, and the warrior returned to Mizpeh, exulting in his success. God had redeemed his people. The thanks and praises of a grateful nation were showered upon his track. The loving father hastened home to enjoy the congratulations of his neighbors, and still more of his daughter—his only child.

Arrived upon the hill which overlooked his dwelling, he halted; for now the full purport of his vow broke in upon his mind. The Lord had "without fail delivered the children of Ammon into his hands;" he had returned in peace to his house, and whatever "came forth of the doors of his house to meet him must be the Lord's to be offered up for a burnt-offering."

It was but for a moment. The door opened as his eye painfully regarded it. It opened, and something came forth; not a pet lamb, not even a servant or a neighbor; but his daughter, his only child, the object in whom his very existence was bound up. "Behold," says the sacred narrative, "his daughter came out to meet him with timbrels and with dances." Jephthah rent his clothes, and in the anguish of his heart cried aloud, "Alas, my daughter! thou hast brought me very low. I have opened my mouth to the Lord, and I cannot go back."

Adah was a daughter in every way worthy

of that warrior sire, the mighty hunter of Gilead. Casting away the instruments of rejoicing, and changing the merry dance to solemn measures, she answered: "My father, if thou hast opened thy mouth unto the Lord, do to me according to that which hath proceeded out of thy mouth." She had but one request to make, and she was ready for the sacrifice. She asked that she might go among the mountains for two months, and there, with the virgins of Israel, prepare her mind to meet in calmness and resignation her impending doom. The request was granted, and during two revolving moons the heroic woman joined in the hymns and prayers of her friends, with which the mountain caves of Gilead became vocal.

When the two months had expired, and the day arrived which was to bring this sad affair to a close, a vast multitude gathered together to witness the event. Precisely as the sun came on the meridian she was seen, followed by a long train of her friends, winding their way down the mountain's side to the fatal spot where the altar was erected, and her father, with an almost broken heart, was standing, prepared to fulfill his vow.

She approached him, and with one long kiss of affection bade him farewell. Taking hold of the thick mourning veil which she wore, he drew it gently over her face and drew his sword. But she rapidly unveiled herself, and said she needed not to have her face covered, for she was not afraid to die. Her father replied that he could not strike the blow while she looked upon him, and again cast it over her. She threw it off the second time, and, turning from him, she said she would look up to the heavens, so that his hand should not be unnerved by the sight of her face, but that she would not consent to die in the dark. A third time, however, he insisted, and a third time she as resolutely cast it off, this time holding the ends of it firmly in her hands, and then in the hearing of the multitude she solemnly declared that if this ceremony was insisted upon she would claim the protection of the law and refuse the fate that otherwise she was willing to endure. She said it was the practice to cover the faces of murderers and criminals when they were about to be put to death, but for her part she was no criminal, and died only to redeem her father's honor. Again she averred that she would cast her eyes upward upon the source of light, and in that position she invited the fatal blow. It fell. Her gentle spirit mounted to the heavens upon which her last gaze had been fixed, and so the deed was consummated which has rendered the name of Jephthah's Daughter forever famous in the annals of Scripture.

For hundreds of years, and even down to the time of Samuel, "it was a custom in Israel that the daughters of Israel went yearly to lament the daughter of Jephthah, the Gileadite, four days in the year."

I will now explain to you the manner of giving the sign of this degree.

SIGN OF DAUGHTER'S DEGREE.

A lady having a veil on, in the usual manner, first pulls it down over her face, then three times in succession raises it, by taking one corner with the right and the other with the left hand, and when lifting it the third time throws the veil over the top of her head, and holding on to the corner looks up. This is called the "Daughter's Sign."

A Mason seeing this sign takes a card, writes his name on one side of it, and on the other writes, "Alas, my daughter" which is the pass. The sign alludes to the refusal of

Jephthah's Daughter to have her face covered when about to be executed.

The pass is used to recall the lamentable but glorious event to which the entire history of Jephthah's daughter refers.

The color blue, belonging to this degree, alludes to the cerulean hue of the mountains in whose solitude Jephthah's Daughter passed two months while preparing herself for death. It signifies Faithfulness, and adjures us to be carefully observant of duty.

The emblems of this degree are the Sword and Veil. The Sword reminds us of the instrument of the death of this noble woman. The Veil signifies her determination to die without fear, and facing the light.

Sister Conductress, will you lead this Sister to the second point of the Star for instruction from Sister Ruth.

[In guiding the candidate from one point of the Star to the other, during the process of initiation, the Conductress leads her around the chair of the officer by whom she has just been instructed, keeping the chair on her right, and then around the Altar, keeping the Altar on her left, then over to the next point. Square corners are always observed in the marches of the Order. Music should be played or sung during the progression from one point to the other, or the Worthy Patron may recite certain Bible verses appropriate to each degree. For the march from Adah to Ruth the selection is Judges 11; 35 and 36. After the Conductress has led the candidate up to Ruth, she says:]

Cond. Sister Ruth, I bring to you our Sister for instruction in the virtue of faithful adherence to religious principles, as illustrated by the Bible story of Ruth.

Ruth. The history of Ruth, as composing a degree of the Eastern Star, is as follows:

Ruth was of the nation of Moab, an idolatrous people. She married a man named Mahlon, formerly a citizen of Bethlehem, who had taken up his residence in the land of Moab, where he died. He was a worshiper of God, and by his pious example and teachings she was converted to the true religion. A few happy years followed, and then the calamity of widowhood came upon her. Upon his death-bed he solemnly exhorted her, for her soul's sake, to leave the dangerous company in which she would be thrown, and go to the city of Bethlehem, where dwelt the people of God.

Immediately after his death she obeyed his pious injunctions. Forsaking her home and friends, she journeyed in company with her aged mother-in-law to Bethlehem, where she arrived in due time, way-worn and so poor that she was compelled, for her own support and that of her friend, to seek some means of securing a livelihood. There was nothing, however, that she could do, save to go into the barley fields—for it was the time of harvest—and glean among the poorest and lowest classes of the people for a support. The very first attempt she made at this labor exhausted her strength. She had been reared in luxury, and the toil was too great for her. The sharp stubble wounded her feet. The blazing sun oppressed her brain. The jeers and insults of her companions alarmed and discouraged her, and long before the hour of noon, with only two little handfuls of barley, as the fruits of her labor, she sought the shade of a tree to rest herself for a few moments before retiring from the field.

At this instant Boaz, the owner of the field, entered. He was a pious and charitable man. None in Bethlehem was so rich, none more beloved and honored than he. As he entered the field, he observed near the gleaners the form of one differing in garb and manners from the rest, and asked the overseer who she was. In reply he learned that she was a woman from Moab, who had asked leave to glean among the sheaves, but that evidently she was unaccustomed to such labor, for she had been there since the sunrise, and had gathered but two little handfuls of barley. This excited the kindly feelings of Boaz, and he went to her to say a word of sympathy, and to offer her relief.

As she saw him approach she supposed him to be the owner of the field, and come to order her away. Ever since the morning she had met nothing but scorn and reproach, and she looked for it now. Raising her hands, therefore, to show him how small were her gleanings, and that she had taken nothing from the sheaves, she placed them meekly upon her breast, as showing her willingness to submit to whatever lot she might be called upon to endure, and cast her eyes upward, as appealing to God against the inhumanity of man. It was for God she had forsaken home, wealth and friends, and the disconsolate widow, alone in the world, had none other to whom she could look for protection. This mute appeal was not lost upon the kind heart of Boaz. He spoke words of sympathy and tenderness to her. He encouraged her to persevere. From the provisions brought for his reapers he bade her eat and drink. He directed that handfuls of barley should be dropped on purpose in her way by the reapers, so that she might gather an ample supply; and when she returned home to her mother-in-law she bore with her enough for their immediate necessities. In a short time Ruth became the wife of Boaz, by whom she had a son called Obed, the father of Jesse, the father of David, the father of Solomon, whose wisdom and power are known to every intelligent Freemason. I will now explain to you the manner of giving the sign of this degree.

SIGN OF WIDOW'S DEGREE.

Take anything convenient, as a handkerchief or newspaper, in each hand, to represent handfuls of barley heads, filling the hands and sticking out a few inches. Then extend the hands in front as if to display their contents, and next cross the wrists on the breast, the contents of each hand pointing upward toward the shoulders, also looking upward. The sign alludes to Ruth holding out two handfuls of barley to Boaz, and appealing mutely to God.

A Mason seeing this sign, writes his name on one side of a card, and on the other writes, "Who is this?" which is the pass of this degree. He then presents her the card.

The pass is used to recall the then lowering but afterwards glorious history of the he oic Ruth.

The color yellow, belonging to this degree, alludes to the ripened grain that composed the barley sheaves of Boaz, among which Ruth was gleaning. It signifies Constanc and teaches respect to religious principles.

The emblem is the Sheaf, reminding us of the liberality of Boaz. From this sign of plenty, composed of many small parts, we are taught that an abundant competence for old age may be secured by habitual diligence, gaining bit by bit, and adding it to the results of earlier efforts.

Sister Conductress, will you lead our Sister to the third point of the Star, there to receive further instruction from Sisther Esther.

[The appropriate verses to be recited here by the Worthy Patron, if music is lacking are from Ruth 2; 4, 5, 6.]

Cond. Sister Esther, I bring to you this Sister for instruction in the praiseworthy quality of faithfulness to family and friends, as illustrated by the history of Esther.

Esther. The history of Esther, as composing a degree of the Eastern Star is thus given:

Her husband, Ahasuerus, otherwise termeα Artaxerxes, was King of Persia, a monarch of vast power, a man faithful to his word, and devotedly attached to the queen-consort.

The heroine, Esther, was a Jewish damsel of the tribe of Benjamin. The family had not returned to Judea after the permission given by Cyrus, and she was born beyond the Tigris, about five hundred years before the Christian era. Her parents being dead, Mordecai, her uncle, took care of her education. After Ahasuerus had divorced Queen Vashti, search was made throughout Persia for the most beautiful women, and Esther was one selected. She found favor in the eyes of the king, who married her with royal magnificence, bestowing largesses and remissions of tribute on his people.

Her matchless beauty having attracted the attention of the king; her virtues secured his love, but her wonderful genius gained his permanent admiration and respect. No woman has ever left behind her a better record of wisdom than Esther. It is a standing tradition among her people that as Solomon was to men so was Esther to women, the wisest of her sex. The more intimately the king became acquainted with her mental powers the more he respected them. There was no problem of state so intricate that she could not aid him to solve. In time she became his confidant, and shared with him in the greatness of the kingdom. These circumstances enabled her in a season of peril to save her nation from destruction.

The enemies of the Jews, who were numerous and powerful, had brought false accusations before the king, and persuaded him to utter an edict that, upon a fixed day, the entire race throughout all Persia should be exterminated. The chosen people of God were doomed to be extirpated from the face of the country. The instrument to avert so great a calamity was the heroine, Esther.

No soon did she learn of this cruel edict than she promptly resolved to save her people or perish in the same destruction. The king had often admitted his indebtedness to her counsels, and pledged his royal word to grant

her any request she might make of him, even
"to the half of the kingdom," and Esther now
resolved to test his sincerity, and appeal to
him, even at the risk of her own life, to re-
verse the horrible edict.   She attired herself
in her white silken robes, placed a brilliant
crown upon her head, gathered her maidens
around her, and went boldly, and in state, to
the palace of the king at Shushan.

It was a day of Grand Council, a gathering
of the governors, princes and officers of Persia.
The dependent nations had sent in their
deputations to pay homage and tribute, and
the royal guards thronged the ante-chambers
of the palace.   It was a standing law of that
place that none should enter the king's presence
without summons, under penalty of death, and
the sentinels as the queen passed reminded her
of this and warned her of her danger.   But
she bade them stand aside, and so, pale but
firm, she passed through the vestibule into the
great council chamber.

The scene was magnificent.   The king upon
his throne of gold and ivory; the gorgeous
equipages of his officers, and the splendor of
the apartment itself, all made up a display
rarely equaled and never surpassed.   Through

all the crowd of courtiers Esther boldly passed, and amidst the deathly silence of the observers stood up before the king. Pale with fasting and sleeplessness, but not with fear, her cheeks emulated the whiteness of her silken robes. She fastened her eye fearlessly upon the king, who, angry at the violation of the law, frowned sternly upon her. It was the crisis of her life. The wise woman felt it to be so, and at once reminded him of his former pledges by a method understood between them. She saw his golden scepter bent toward her, and hastened to secure her pardon by coming forward, kneeling, and laying her hand upon it. Graciously said the king, "What wilt thou, Queen Esther? and what is thy request?" It shall be given thee even unto the half of thy kingdom. The admiring crowds applauded the generosity of their monarch, and as he placed her beside him on the throne, gave utterance to loud expression of admiration at her beauty, discretion, and favor with the king.

The sacred narrative informs us of the consummate tact with which Esther pursued the advantage she had gained. She achieved a complete success and saved the nation, which, to this day, keeps an annual festival in her honor.

I will now explain to you the manner of giving the sign of this degree.

Place open right hand just above top of head, then throw hand forward and upward, palm out, and height of the eyes, then lay open hand on the breast.

The sign alludes to the manner of Queen Esther's appearance before King Ahasuerus, as explained in the history of the degree.

A Mason seeing this sign writes on one side of a card his name, and on the other side, "What wilt thou?" which is the pass of this degree, and presents the card to the lady.

The pass is used to recall the grand sacrifice and triumphant success of the heroic Esther.

The color appropriate to this degree is white, alluding to the silken robes of Esther, symbolic of the spotless purity of her character. It teaches us that a chaste and worthy life is beyond censure.

The emblem, the crown and scepter united, reminds us of the queenly state of Esther, and of the manner in which she hailed the king. It is a sign of royalty and power.

Sister Conductress, you will continue with

our sister to the fourth point of the star, for instruction from Martha.

[The appropriate verses to be recited here by the Worthy Patron. in the absence of music, are Esther 5; 2, 3.]

Cond. Sister Martha, I present this sister before you for instruction in the hope of immortality, and in the moral qualities of trust and faith in the time of trouble, as portrayed in the history of Martha.

Martha. The history of Martha, as comprising a degree of the Eastern Star, is thus given:

Her brother, Lazarus, was a resident of Bethany, a man of good standing among his fellow-citizens, and the friend of Jesus Christ.

The family, composed of two sisters, Martha and Mary, with their brother Lazarus, seem to have possessed all things needful for a happy life. Bound up in the love of each other, and blessed with the friendship of him whom to know is "everlasting life," the little group were distinguished from their neighbors by a name that proved how thoroughly their hearts were occupied with divine things. They were "the beloved of the Master. the happy household of Bethany."

Upon an occasion when their divine guest had gone out, beyond the Jordan, upon a mission of charity, Lazarus was taken suddenly and violently ill. The terrified sisters hastened to inform Jesus of the fact by a messenger, who was instructed to say, "Lord, behold he whom thou lovest is sick!" They reasonably supposed that so tender a missive could not fail to success. But the Saviour returned an ambiguous reply. The "Beloved at Bethany" died and was buried. Four days passed, days shrouded with mourning, still the Saviour returned not. The sisters were abandoned to grief, not alone for the loss of their brother, their only earthly protector, but for the unkindness of him upon whom they had leaned as the "Rock of their salvation." Yet Martha retained her faith, and trusted in him yet to come and restore the friend they had lost.

At the close of the fourth day, intelligence reached them that Jesus was returning to Bethany. Martha hastened to meet him, fell on her knees before him, raised her hands imploringly toward His face, and with deep emotion cried aloud: "Lord, if Thou hadst been here, my brother had not died!" Looking a moment after into His face, and animated by the God-like benignity with which He looked down upon her, she added: "But I know that even now whatsoever Thou wilt ask of God, He will give it Thee!"

Amazing faith, heroic spirit of confidence in her friend! Though her brother had been four days in the embraces of death, and the subject of its corrupting influences—though the weight of watchfulness and sorrow rested heavily upon her spirit as she knelt, her hands wildly raised to heaven—there was a spirit of prophecy in her words which gives them a value altogether their own.

Then Jesus said: "Thy brother shall rise again"—testing her faith still further.

She replied: "I know that he shall rise again in the resurrection at the last day."

Jesus said unto her, "I am the resurrection and the life; he who believeth in me, though he were dead, yet shall he live; and whosoever liveth and believeth in me shall never die. Believest thou this?"

Martha answered at once in the tone and spirit of perfect faith: "Yea Lord, I believe that Thou art the Christ, the Son of God, which should come into the world!"

The reward of such faith was soon rendered. Taking her by the hand, and passing by their dwelling, where they were joined by Mary, they went to the sepulchre, and, as every reader of Scripture knows, Jesus raised the dead man to life.

I will now explain to you the manner of giving the sign of this degree.

SIGN OF SISTER'S DEGREE.

Join the hands together at the tips of thumbs and fingers, forming the figure of a triangle. Raise the triangle thus formed directly above the eyes. Raise the eyes, looking through the triangle.

The sign alludes to the appeal of Martha on first meeting Christ after the death of her brother Lazarus. A Mason seeing this sign writes his name on one side of a card, and on the other writes, "Believest thou this?" which is the pass of this degree. He then hands the lady the card.

The pass will recall the spirit of fidelity which characterizes the history of Martha.

The color for this degree is green, alluding to the resurrection of Lazarus, and, by direct inference, to that final and grander resurrection in the last day. Never does Freemason cast the evergreen sprig into the open grave of his brother but the coming event is thus beautifully fore-shadowed.

The Broken Column is an emblem of the death of a young man in the vigor of life, and calls attention to the uncertainty of temporal existence.

Sister Conductress, you will lead this sister to the fifth point of the star, for further instruction from Sister Electa.

[They proceed in the regular way to the fifth point. The verses which may be used here instead of music are John 11; 21-26.]

Cond. Sister Electa, I present before you this sister for instruction in the estimable virtue of fortitude in bearing wrongs and injustice for the sake of Truth, as portrayed in the story of Electa.

Electa. The history of Electa, as composing a degree of the Order of the Eastern Star is thus given: It deals with the story of a person whose confidence in God's justice gave her perfect patience and submission amidst the most inhuman wrongs. She is alluded to in the Second Epistle of John, as "the elect lady and her children."

She was a lady of high repute in the land

of Judea, of noble family, wealthy and accomplished, who lived in the days of St. John the
Evangelist, and was remarkable for her pro-
fuse benevolence to the poor.

Electa had been reared, as all her neighbors
were, a heathen. The idols of Rome were the
only gods she knew. Like Ruth, however, she
had been preserved from the abominations of
the system, and when by good fortune she was
enabled to hear from inspired lips the story
of Calvary and its Divine victim, her heart
readily opened to the influences of the Holy
Spirit. She became converted, together with
her husband and all her household. She even
professed, before the world, her faith in the
despised Nazarene, though well she knew that
to do so was to expose herself to reproaches,
to persecution, and haply to death.

Fourteen years, however, passed away before that great trial came upon her. These
years became the happier as well as the better
years of her life. She gave her great income
to the relief of the poor. Her splendid mansion
was made a house of abode to weary and
persecuted pilgrims. The poorest of the flock,
the tattered and foot-sore beggar, coming up
the great avenue to her door, was met as the

father met his prodigal son. She ran out hastily to meet him, took him warmly by the hand, and welcomed him. She led him to the best apartment, refreshed him with the richest wine in a golden cup, fed, cheered, clothed her guest, nor suffered him to depart until he was strengthened for the journey. Through all the country her name was famous as "the beneficent and affectionate Electa." And all this time she was ripening for the better world, and preparing for a fate which, although protracted, was inevitably to settle upon her.

The time of her martyrdom drew nigh. A great persecution began, and any one who had confessed the name of Jesus was required to recant from his faith, or suffer the penalty of the law. Electa was visited by a band of soldiers, whose chief officer proposed the test of casting a cross on the ground and putting her foot upon it, whereupon he would report her recantation. She refused, and instead of throwing down the crucifix, clasped it to her breast, showing her faith in her Saviour and her readiness to die for him rather than deny him. The family were then cast into a dungeon and kept there one year. Then the Roman Judge came and offered her another opportunity to recant, promising that if she would do so she should be protected. Again she refused, and this brought the drama to a speedy close. The whole family were scourged to the very verge of death. They were then drawn on a cart, by oxen, to the nearest hill and crucified. She saw her husband perish. She saw each of her sons and daughters die on the cruel tree. She was then nailed there, and being about to pass to the better land, she prayed with her expiring breath, "Father, forgive them, for they know not what they do!"

The color red belonging to this degree symbolizes fervency, and alludes to the noble generosity of Electa, displayed toward the poor and persecuted of her faith.

The emblem of the Cup reminds us of the ardent hospitality of Electa, excited by the view of poverty and distress.

I will now explain to you the manner of giving the sign of this degree.

Hands crossed on the breast as if clasping something to her bosom, at the same time looking up.

The sign alludes to Electa's clasping the crucifix to her bosom, representing her love for the Saviour.

A Mason seeing this sign writes his name on one side of a card, and on the other writes, "Love one another," which is the pass of this degree.

The pass is used to recall the summing up of the grand tragedy which crowned the life of the heroic Electa.

Sister Conductress, you will lead our sister before the Worthy Patron for further instruction.

[Carrying out the idea of a labyrinth as before, the Conductress leads the candidate around to the Worthy Patron. In the absence of music the Worthy Patron may recite Second John 1; 3, 5, 6, and First John 4; 7, 10.]

Cond. Worthy Patron, again I bring before you this sister who has proceeded through the labyrinthian mazes of our Order. At each point of our Star she has received instruction in the exalted virtues shown in the lives of those illustrious women whom the members of our Order strive to emulate.

W. P. We welcome you with true pleasure, and urge you to unite with us zealously in our good works. The Worthy Matron will now address you.

W. M. In behalf of .... Chapter I heartily welcome you, my sister. I desire to inform you as to your true relationship to the Masonic fraternity. A little knowledge of the real nature and purposes of Masonry will help you to understand this. We are not a part of the Masonic institution, yet we are connected with Masonry by intimate and tender ties. The widow and orphan daughter of a Master Mason take the place of the husband and father in the affections and good deeds of the lodge. If their character in unjustly assailed, the brethren are in duty bound to protect them. If they are in want, distressed for the necessities of life, the brethren will divide their means with them. If, traveling at a distance from home they find themselves sick and in want, among strangers, they have but to make themselves known as the widow and orphan daughter of a worthy Master Mason, and lo, the hand of relief is stretched out toward them. The kind voice of sympathy is heard to cheer them. They are no longer strangers, but friends, dear friends, and thus they are constrained to bless that society, whose kind deeds are not confined to the narrow limits of home.

This is what has happened, what is happening every day. The widow has been provided with a home, her children educated and reared up to honorable stations, her own heart cheered and comforted by the blessed influences of Masonry.

These, then, are the reasons why we think that members of the Order of the Eastern Star should be the most devoted friends that Masonry possesses. To us are given all the advantages of the society, its shield of protection, its hand of relief, and its voice of sympathy. The only Masonic privilege denied to us is that of visiting the lodge. Women cannot be made Masons. This is a rule that has been handed down with other rules of Masonry for thousands of years. Each Mason present pledged himself before he was admitted into the lodge that he would never allow any of the ancient rules of Masonry to be changed, and this is one of them. Therefore Masons cannot invite us to visit their lodges. But, as I have said, they can, and do, and will share with us in all the solid privileges and benefits of Masonry, and thus practically unite us with them in this great, this glorious, this heavenly work of doing good.

We, the mothers, wives, sisters, daughters and widows of Masons join with them in their good works, generously giving of our goods, our time and our sympathy.

You my sister have now been received into our Order, and this opportunity for service is yours. You have taken upon yourself the Obligation of the Order; you have received instruction in the principles upon which the order is based. May you find true happiness in our fraternal love and companionship, and zealous devotion to our aims and efforts.

We are united in an earnest purpose, for which we implore Divine aid and counsel. Let us bow before our Heavenly Father, praying for His Help and blessing.

[With three gavel blows the Worthy Patron calls the members to rise, and the Chaplain offers the following prayer: * * *]

PRAYER.

Thou Source of all wisdom, truth and love, grant us, we pray, that in receiving this person into our Order we may also receive added strength and grace. May the golden chain thus lengthened become brighter for this added link, and be made stronger to accomplish our great work. Increase our strength to serve mankind and to do Thy will, with all honor to Thee. And when one by one these links shall fall away in death, may the parting be but temporary, and the meeting for all time. In that world where there is no death may we know the deep happiness of loving and serving Thee forever. Amen.

Members. So may it be.

[If desired an ode may be sung after the prayer.)

The Worthy Patron then seats the Chapter, with one gavel blow,* and the initiation ceremonies are continued.]

W. P. In assuming the solemn pledges of this Order, you, my sister, are beginning a new period of your existence. Henceforward you will be known as one of the members of this Order whose inspiration is the Star of Bethlehem, directing all the faithful to that city not made with hands, the New Jerusalem.

Let me remind you that privileges bring their obligations. You have been told that we labor together in love and fellowship, devoted to good works for each other and for our neighbors, that through our Order may be extended help, relief, and true sympathy to the needy and sorrowing.

At the five points of the Star you have heard the histories of those noble women whose characters furnish us with worthy examples:— of that heroic daughter of Jephthah, doomed to die for her father's sake; of Ruth, the harvest gleaner in the field of Boaz, who forsook all things to dwell among the people of God; of Esther, that noble daughter of bondage, who so bravely resolved to share the fortunes of the exiles of Israel; of Martha, mourning the loss of her dearly beloved brother; and finally, of that devoted philanthropist, Electa, who above all women suffered for her Master's sake the loss of home, family, wealth, and life itself.

You have taken upon yourself our solemn Obligation: you have received instruction in certain secrets of our Order, which will enable you to recognize the members, and to make yourself known as a member of the Order. That these secret signs and passes may be fully understood by you I will explain them, and give the regular form of examination, by which you may prove your membership. The Conductress will assist by demonstrating the signs, and answering the questions properly.

W. P. Are you a member of the Order of

the Eastern Star!

Cond. We have seen His star in the East.

W. P. For what came you here?

Cond. And are come to worship Him.

W. P. Have you the cabalistic word?

Cond. I have.

W. P. Will you give it to me?

Cond. I will, with your assistance.

W. P. Begin.

Cond. No, you begin.

W. P. Begin you.

Cond. F.

W. P. A.

Cond. T.

W. P. A.

Cond. L. Fatal.

W. P. Has that word any significance?

Cond. It has, two. First, that it would be fatal to the character of any lady for truth, who should disclose the secrets of these degrees unlawfully. Second, each of the letters of this word stands for one or more words, which words make the cabalistic motto.

W. P. Have you the cabalistic motto?

Cond. I have.

W. P. Will you give it to me?

Cond. I will, with your assistance.

W. P. Begin.

Cond. No. you begin.

W. P. Begin you.

Cond. Fairest.

W. P. Among.

Cond. Thousands.

W. P. Altogether.

Cond. Lovely. Fairest among thousands, altogether lovely.

W. P. Jephthah's daughter, because she cheerfully rendered up her life to preserve her father's honor, was fairest among thousands, altogether lovely. Ruth, because she forsook home, friends and wealth, that she might dwell among the people of God, was fairest among thousands, altogether lovely. Esther, because she was prepared to resign her crown and life to save the people of God from death or to perish with them, was fairest among thousands, altogether lovely. Martha, because amidst sickness, death and loneliness, she never for a moment doubted the Saviour's power to raise the dead, was fairest among thousands, altogether lovely. And finally, Electa, because she joyfully rendered up home, husband, children, good name and life, that she might testify to her Christian love, by a martyr's death, was fairest among thousands, altogether lovely.

So let it be with you, my sister. As you illustrate the virtues of these chosen and tried servants of God, so shall be your reward. You may not be called to suffer as they did, and yet sufferings and trials await all of us in this sublunary state; and those who in the place to which they are called best endure these trials, and resist temptations, prove that had they lived in ancient times they would not have been found wanting, although called to endure as a ruth or an Electa.

I will now explain the signs, and the Conductress will illustrate them.

The first is the Daughter's sign, or the Sign of Jephthah's daughter. It is made by three motions. First cover the face with a veil or handkerchief.

1. Take the veil in the hands at the lower corners, raising it as high as the forehead.

2. Drop and raise it again as before.

3. Drop and raise it as before, then throw it over the head to the back of the neck, holding the ends firmly in the hands.

This sign represents the refusal of Jephthah's daughter to have her face covered when about to be executed.

The PASS. "Alas, my daughter!" A member on seeing the Daughter's Sign should make this response.

The Widow's Sign, or the Sign of Ruth, is made by three motions. Take in each hand something to represent a handful of barley straw.

1. Let the hands hang perpendicularly at the sides. Then raise them and hold them out horizontally forward, the elbows pressing against the sides of the body, as if showing the barley straw.

2. Bring the hands nearly side by side on the breast, a little way under the chin, letting the heads of the barley straw (or their substitute) fall gracefully over the shoulders.

3. Cast the eyes upward.

This sign represents Ruth holding out two handfuls of barley to Boaz, and appealing mutely to God.

The PASS. "Who is this?" A member on seeing the Widow's Sign should respond with these words.

The Wife's Sign, or the Sign of Esther is made by three motions.

1. Raise the right hand, the palm downward, a little over the head, as if touching a crown there.

2. Throw the hand forward, as if touching a scepter held by the person opposite; keep the hand level with the eyes.

3. Carry the hand to the left breast.

This sign represents Queen Esther's appearance before King Ahasuerus as explained in the history of the degree.

The PASS. "What wilt thou?" A member on seeing the Wife's Sign should respond with these words.

The Sister's Sign, or the Sign of Martha is made by three motions.

1. Join the hands together at the tips of the thumbs and fingers, forming the figure of a triangle.

2. Raise the triangle thus formed directly above the eyes.

3. Raise the eyes, looking through the triangle.

This sign represents Martha appealing to Christ, after the death of her brother Lazarus.

The PASS. "Believest thou this?" A member on seeing this Sister's Sign, should respond with these words.

The Mother's Sign, or the Sign of Electa is made by two motions.

1. Cross the arms over the breast, the left arm over the right, the ends of the fingers on the shoulders.

2. Cast the eyes upward.

This sign represents Electa clasping the crucifix to her bosom, depicting her love for the Saviour.

The SIGN OF SALUTATION is given by any member entering or leaving the Chapter room during the work of the Chapter. To give it the member advances past the Associate Matron toward the Altar, facing the East, clasps the hands with the fingers interlaced, makes a slight bow and goes to her seat or retires, as the case may be.

The PASS. "Love one another!" A member on seeing the Mother's Sign should respond with these words.

The GRIP of our Order is given in two motions.

1. Take the right hand of the person opposite, in the ordinary manner of shaking hands.

2. Move the thumb to the fleshy part of the hand, between the thumb and forefinger, and give a slight pressure.

The GRAND HONORS are made thus: Cross the arms over the breast, the right arm over the left, the ends of the fingers resting on the shoulders; make a bow.

I will now explain the Signet of our Order, which is designed to assist the memory of any

who have received the degrees of the Order of the Eastern Star. You will observe that the star in the Signet is five-pointed, representing the five degrees of the Order. In the different points of the star will be seen the symbols of the five characters, Jephthah's Daughter, Ruth, Esther, Martha and Electa, whose histories make up the degrees. Each point has its distinctive color, and emblematic flowers, as follows:

Jephthah's Daughter, blue, for faithfulness, represented by the violet.

Ruth, yellow, for steadfastness, represented by the jasmine.

Esther, white, for pure happiness and light, represented by the lily.

Martha, green, for hope in immortality, represented by the fern.

Electa, red, for zeal, represented by the red rose.

The central division of the Signet, or the center of the star, is divided into five parts, bearing emblems alluding to the distinguished characters composing the degrees, as follows:

1. The Open Bible is appropriate to Jephthah's Daughter as the symbol of obedience to the word of God.

2. The Bunch of Lilies is appropriate to Ruth, as the Lily of the Valley.

3. The Sun is appropriate to Esther, as the effulgent sun is the symbol of crowned majesty.

4. The Lamb is appropriate to Martha, as the symbol of innocence, faith and humility.

5. The Lion is appropriate to Electa, as the symbol of the courage and strength which sustained her during her severe trials.

Around the outer edge of this central division of the Signet will be noted the letters forming the cabalistic word, F A T A L.

And now my sister, you have been duly initiated into our Order. As we unite in the noble purposes of the Order, may each member be found "fairest among thousands, altogether lovely."

You will now be led by the Conductress to the desk of the Secretary, where you will sign the By-laws, and then return to this present position.

[Music may be played while the new member
signs the By-laws. She is then led to the outer
room, where she takes off any robes or special
paraphernalia which she may have been given
for the initiation ceremonies. A badge of the
Order is put on her, and she is conducted back to
her place in the East. The Chapter is called up
• • • and all join in a song of welcome.]

WELCOME

A welcome and a greeting now,
  To gentle friends and sisters true,
Around the place where Masons bow,
  And pay their homage due;
On chequered floor, 'neath starry sky,
Welcome kind friends of Masonry!.

To her who finds a Father here,
  Or Brother's strong and trusty hand;
To her who mourns the lost and dear,
  Once cherished in our band;
To her who husband's love doth own,
Greeting and wisdom every one!

Welcome the light our emblems shed,
  Welcome the hopes yon volume gives—
Welcome the love our covenants spread,
  The wages each receives;
And when is past life's toilsome week,
Welcome the home that Masons seek.

W. P. Members of .... Chapter, No. ...., let us now extend a hearty welcome to this sister who has received the degrees of our Order, and whose initiation has been completed satisfactorily to us, and we hope to her. You are now at liberty to engage in a social hour until called to order by the sound of the gavel, for the closing ceremonies.

INSTALLATION OF OFFICERS

After the regular annual elections, there should be a formal installation of the officers who have been elected by a majority vote. The installation ceremonies may take place either at a regular or a special meeting. They may be held in public, in which case the secret work of the opening ceremonies may be omitted; or the Chapter may be opened in private in the Chapter room, the Chapter adjourning to the Lodge Hall for the installation. An address should then be made on the history and aims of the Order.

The first officers of a new Chapter must be installed by a Grand Matron, or a Grand Patron, or someone deputized to take their places. These officers may also conduct the annual installation of officers, or this may be in charge of a present or Past Worthy Matron or Worthy Patron.

The Installing Officer takes the chair and appoints a Marshal to assist in the installation. If the Installing Officer is a Grand Officer, the Marshal will be Grand Marshal. The officers will have to be addressed by their proper titles, such changes as are necessary being made in the wording of the ceremonies as given here. If the former Warder and Sentinel have both been reelected a Brother must be appointed to stand at the door during the installation. The Marshal gathers up the various badges of office, ready for use, and also gets the list of newly elected officers from the Secretary.

After the address on the Order of the Eastern Star, its history and principles, the installation ceremonies are begun by the officer in charge, whom for convenience we will here designate as the Installing Officer.

Inst. Officer. Members of the Order of the Eastern Star, it is a significant occasion in the history of our Chapter when our newly elected officers assume their responsibilities. Let us implore the Divine blessing and counsel before beginning the ceremony of installation.

[The Chapter rises. * * *]

PRAYER

(By the Chaplain or the Installing Officer)

Our Heavenly Father, all-wise and good, let Thy blessing descend upon us as we are here assembled to perform our duties. We acknowledge the limitations of human effort, and call upon Thee for strength and support. Guide and direct these officers upon whom will now devolve the responsibility of governing this Chapter. Give them wisdom and power, and trust in Thy protection. May the work of our Order be blessed and prospered, and may our labors progress in peace and concord, to Thy honor and glory. Amen.

Members. So may it be.

[The Chapter is seated. *]

Inst. Officer. Sister Marshal, you will now call up the officers elect who will stand on the other side of the altar, facing me, ready to take the obligation of office.

[In response to the roll call by the Marshal the newly elected officers take their places according to rank, in a semi-circle facing the East.]

Inst. Officer. Members of .... Chap. No. ....,....., Order of the Eastern Star, you see before you the officers whom you have chosen to serve during the coming year. You will rise while they receive the obligation.

• • •

Officers elect, do you solemnly pledge your-selves to the faithful and conscientious per-formance of the duties pertaining to your re-spective offices,. and to observe the general rules of this Order, and those of this Chapter?

[The officers answer in the affirmative. The Chapter is seated. * The Marshal brings up the

Worthy Matron to the Installing Officer, and says]

M. Worthy ...., I take pleasure in presenting Sister ....for installation as Worthy Matron of our Chapter for the coming year. Our sister realizes fully the important and responsible nature of her duties as Worthy Matron, but she is willing to accept the responsibility with the honor. She confidently hopes that through the help of the members, and by the grace of God, she may be able to fulfill her duties worthily.

Inst. Officer. Sister, before proceeding further it will be necessary for you to signify your concurrence with those regulations of our Order upon the strict observance of which depends the success and permanency of our obligation.

You admit that the name of The Order of the Eastern Star, the character of the Order and the means of recognition are unchangeable?

Ans. I do.

You admit that a belief in the existence of a Supreme Being is essential for membership in this Order?

Ans. I do.

You promise to comply with the laws and regulations of the Grand Chapter, and also the by-laws of this Chapter, and to allow no infraction of them by the members?

Ans. I do.

You admit that no new Chapter can be organized without permission in the form of a Charter or Dispensation from the Grand Chapter having jurisdiction over the territory in which the new Chapter is formed? And that no Chapter illegally formed shall be sanctioned by our Order, and none of the members of such a Chapter shall be recognized as members of this Order?

Ans. I do.

You agree that no visitor shall be permitted in this Chapter during secret work unless duly examined and found to be legally entitled to be present; and that no person shall be admitted who is apt to disturb the peace and concord of the Chapter?

Ans. I do.

You agree that a Master Mason in good standing must always preside over the initiation ceremonies?

Ans. I do.

You promise to secure the enforcement of

the rules and regulations of our order to the best of your ability; to strive for the prosperity of our Chapter and to render in every way possible that honorable service which may be expected of the Worthy Matron?

Ans. I do.

Members of .... Chap. No. ...., do you, after hearing the pledges of Sister ...., promise to encourage and uphold her in the duties of her office?

Ans. We do.

Sister ...., the office of Worthy Matron is a responsible position, demanding devoted labor and attention, as well as tact, patience and Wisdom. The members of your Chapter will expect you to counsel them not only in the affairs of the Chapter, but also in their personal cares. They will look to you for advice and sympathy at all times. I need not say that much social grace will be required for the performance of the duties which will devolve upon you.

You will need to be discreet in doing your work, courteous and helpful at all times: punctual and orderly, setting a good example in the matters in which you expect the members to obey you.

Within the Chapter it will be your duty to see that the regular meetings are held; that special meetings shall be called when necessary for the good of the Chapter; that your subordinate officers fill their places with honor and usefulness; that the rules, regulations and by-laws be firmly adhered to; that the funds, records, rituals and other possessions of the Chapter be properly preserved by the officers having them in charge; that the cry of the widow and orphan shall never be ignored and that this Chapter shall fail in none of the aims for which it was established.

You, as Worthy Matron, should strive for the accomplishment of all these purposes, knowing that in electing you to this exalted office your brothers and sisters have placed perfect confidence in your ability.

Sister Marshal, you will now invest our sister with the insignia of her office.

The badge of the Worthy Matron is the Gavel within the Star. It is an emblem of authority and admonishes you that upon your judgment and discretion rests the government of this Chapter, and very largely the prosperity of our organization.

Sister Marshal, you will now conduct our sister to the station of the Worthy Matron, where she will receive the salute of honor from the membership.

[The Installing Officer signals the Chapter to rise * * * and they salute the Worthy Matron with the Grand Honors. The Chapter is Installing Officer.]

The Worthy Matron is given a chair near the Installing Officer.

M, Worthy ...., it gives me pleasure to present to you for installation Brother ...., who has been elected Worthy Patron of this Chapter for the coming year. In electing him to this office the members have expressed their confidence in his zeal and devotion to our cause, and in his ability to contribute to the honor and welfare of our organization.

Inst. Officer. Brother ...., you have heard the 'pledges which the Worthy Matron made before her installation into office. Do you promise that you will also faithfully obey all of those regulations?

Ans. I do.

Inst. Officer. My Brother, you have been

elected to one of the most important offices of our Chapter, and your election is the highest honor which the members can confer upon any Brother. Although from the nature of the order you are not its first officer, yet you will be expected to watch carefully over the interests of the Chapter and to see that the members render prompt obedience to the rules and regulations of the Order.

It is your duty to preside over the initiation ceremonies, and at any other time at the request of the Worthy Matron, to see that the ritual work of the Order is correctly given and that the officers are carefully instructed as to their duties.

You will act as the Worthy Matron's lawful counsellor, supervising the affairs of the Chapter—advising, making decisions, serving as a splendid example of all that is demanded of a worthy member of our Order.

Sister Marshal, you will now invest Brother ....with the insignia of his office.

Inst. Officer. The badge of the Worthy Patron is the Square and Compass within the Star, an emblem of the bond existing between the Masonic Fraternity and the

Order of the Eastern Star. It admonishes you to be always faithful to your obligations to this Order.

Sister Marshal, you will conduct Brother .... to the station of the Worthy Patron, at the left of the Worthy Matron. You will then bring up the Associate Matron elect for installation.

M. Worthy ...., it gives me pleasure to present for installation Sister ...., who has been elected to the office of Associate Matron of our Chapter for the coming year.

Inst. Officer. Sister ...., the duties of your position are indicated by the name of your office. You are the assistant of the Worthy Matron in all branches of her responsible trust, and in her absence you will succeed to all of her privileges as well as to her duties. In order that you may fill that office with credit to yourself and honor to the Chapter it will be necessary for you to familiarize yourself with all its obligations and requirements.

Sister Marshal, you will now invest Sister .... with her badge of office.

Inst. Officer. The badge of the Associate Matron is the Sun within the Star, an emblem of radiance, admonishing you that as the sun brightens the day so should the principles of our Order shine through our lives for the benefit of humanity.

Sister Marshal, you will now conduct Sister ....to the station of the Associate Matron, in the West, and then bring up the Treasurer elect for installation.

M. Worthy ...., it gives me pleasure to present for installation Sister ...., who has been elected Treasurer of this Chapter for the coming year.

Inst. Officer. Sister .... the preservation of the funds of our Chapter requires absolute honesty and care upon the part of the treasurer. The money which will be placed in your hands may be needed for charitable work or for the regular expenses of our Chapter at the most unexpected times. Sister Marshal, you will invest Sister ....with her badge of office.

Inst. Officer. The badge of the Treasurer is the Cross-Keys within the Star, an emblem of security. It admonishes you to be faithful to your trust, in order that the Chapter may meet its necessary expenses and accomplish its works of charity.

Sister Marshal, you will now conduct Sister .... to the Treasurer's station in the Northeast, and then bring up the Secretary for installation.

M. Worthy ...., it gives me pleasure to present Sister ...., Secretary elect of this Chapter for the coming year.

Inst. Officer. Sister ...., yours is an arduous and very responsible trust. Your duty is to make note in proper order of the business transacted at our meetings; to collect all money due the Chapter; to prepare and forward to the Grand Secretary all the necessary returns required by the Constitution, and to conduct all correspondence. Failure to do your duty would complicate and embarrass all of our proceedings and give us a disgraceful record on the books of the Grand Chapter.

Sister Marshal, you will now invest Sister
.............................with her badge of office.

The badge of the Secretary is the Cross-Pens within the Star, an emblem of intelligence, admonishing you to be loyal to your obligations, careful of the accounting of the money which shall p a s s through your hands, and zealous in recording the good deeds of your associates in this Order.

Sister Marshal, you will now conduct Sister .... to the station of the Secretary in the Southeast, and then bring up the Conductress and the Associate Conductress elect for installation.

M. Worthy ...., it gives me pleasure to present Sister ...., Conductress elect, and Sister ...., Associate Conductress elect, for installation into the respective offices in our Chapter to which they have been elected for the coming year.

Inst. Officer. My sisters, upon you falls the task of preparing and conducting through our initiation ceremonies those who seek the privileges of our Order. It is important, therefore, that you should fully understand all of our work; that you should be familiar with the ritual and with the initiation ceremonies. The candidate enters our Chapter with the expectation of receiving a favorable impression of our mysteries and aims. If you present these matters in the right manner, enveloping your official proceedings with sisterly courtesy and dignity, the candidate will acquire a true regard and fondness for this beautiful Order. Remember then that the good impression of our Order which the candidate should receive in initiation may be influenced largely by the way in which you perform your duties.

Sister Marshal, you will now invest our sisters with the badges of their respective offices.

Sister Conductress, t h e badge of your office is the Scroll and Baton within the Star, an emblem of order and guidance. It admonishes you that the first impressions made upon a candidate are lasting, and should always be favorable.

Sister Associate Conductress, the badge of your office is the Baton within the Star, an emblem of control. It admonishes you that good discipline is indispensable to the success of our Order.

Sister Marshal, you will now conduct our sisters to their respective stations in the South and North, and you will then present the Chaplain for installation.

M. Worthy ...., it gives me pelasure to present ...., appointed as Chaplain of our Chapter for the coming year.

Inst. Officer. My brother (or sister) we realize our need of Divine assistance at all times in our labors, and frequently appeal to our Heavenly Father for his blessing. The Chaplain's duty is to conduct the devotions of our Chapter, ministering at the altar as required.

Sister Marshal, you will now invest.............. with ....badge of office.

The badge of office for the Chaplain is the Bible within the Star, representing the Word of God. It admonishes you to conduct yourself worthily, in favor with God and man.

Sister Marshal, you will conduct our Chaplain to .... proper station in the East, on the right of the Worthy Matron. You will then present the Marshal for installation.

M. Worthy ...., it gives me pleasure to present Sister ...., who has been appointed Marshal for the coming year.

Inst. Officer. Sister ...., the office of Marshal is a responsible and honorable position. It is your duty to conduct and marshal all of our processions, to assist in all of our public and private ceremonies; to conduct and announce the officers at the installation ceremonies and to perform any other duties pertaining to your office.

Sister Marshal, you will now invest our Sister with her badge of office.

The badge of the Marshal is the Crossed Batons within the Star, an emblem of guidance. It admonishes you to be courteous and prompt in the discharge of your duties.

Sister Marshal, you will now conduct our Sister to her proper station in the Southeast. You will then present the Organist for installation.

M. Worthy ...., it gives me pleasure to present Sister ...., who has been appointed Organist for the coming year.

Inst. Officer. Sister ...., the name of your office indicates your duties. Faithfulness to your trust will help in rendering the ceremonies of our Chapter impressive, and effective.

Sister Marshal, you will now invest Sister ....with her badge of office.

The badge of office of the Organist is the Lyre within the Star, an emblem of musical and poetic art.. It admonishes you that the impressions of our mystic rites will be more lasting when accompanied by music.

Sister Marshal, you will now conduct our Organist to her station.

Inst. Officer. Sister Marshal, you will present for installation the Warder and Sentinel of our Chapter.

M. Worthy ...., it gives me pleasure to present for installation Sister ...., appointed Warder, and Brother ...., appointed Sentinel for the coming year.

Inst. Officer. Sister .... and Brother ...., you are respectively the inner and outer guards of our Chapter. Upon you, then, we depend for the preservation of that secrecy which is essential to our proceedings, and for protection from untimely alarms which might disturb the solemnity of our ceremonies. Be always on guard, watchful to preserve the peace and harmony of all the meetings of our Chapter.

Sister Marshal, you will now invest Sister ....and Brother ....with their badges of office.

Sister ...., the badge of office of the Warder is the Dove within the Star, an emblem of peace. It admonishes you that the peace and harmony which you help preserve in our Chapter are essential to its success.

Brother ...., the badge of the Sentinel is the Cross-Swords within the Star, an emblem of protection. It admonishes you that upon your watchful care depends our safety from interruption.

Sister Marshal, you will now conduct our Sister and Brother to their respective stations within and without the door, after which you will present for installation the five sisters chosen to represent the five rays of Our Central Star.

M. Worthy ...., it is a pleasure to present the sisters who have been chosen to represent the five rays of our Star: Sister ...., appointed to represent the blue ray of Adah; Sister ...., the yellow ray of Ruth; Sister ...., the white ray of Esther; Sister ...., the green ray of Martha and Sister ...., the red ray of Electa.

Inst. Officer (who may here present each star officer with flowers of the color appropriate to that ray of the Star which she represents). My Sisters, you are the floral center of our Chapter and it is your duty to teach impressively the lessons which the beautiful colors and floral emblems of our Star symbolize, as well as the sublime virtues of those noble women whom you personate in our Rite.

It is important that in the performance of your official duties you should endeavor to envelop all that you say and do with an air of beauty and solemnity, so that from the Central Star of our Chapter, as represented in you, you may emanate a light that will instruct and bring happiness to all those who attend our meetings.

Sister Marshal, you will now invest our sisters with the badges of their respective offices.

Sister Adah, the badge of your office is the Sword and Veil within the Triangle, symbolic of the heroism of Jephthah's Daughter.

Sister Ruth, the badge of your office is the Sheaf within the Triangle, symbolic of the abundance which is the reward of diligence.

Sister Esther, the badge of your office is the Crown and Scepter within the Triangle, symbolic of royalty and power, and reminding you of the unselfish devotion of Queen Esther to her own people.

Sister Martha, the badge of your office is the Broken Column within the Triangle, symbolic of life's uncertainty, and reminding you of the comfort which Martha received from her unswerving faith in God in the time of her sorrow.

Sister Electa, the badge of your office is the Cup within the Triangle, symbolic of the charity and hospitality which we learn from the history of Electa.

These, my sisters, are some of the lessons which are taught by your badges of office. The exalted virtues illustrated in the lives of those illustrous women whom you represent are worthy of emulation. I trust that as you teach these virtues to others in the work of our Order, you will remember also to let them be reflected from your own lives. Thus you will honor the offices to which you have been appointed, and lay up for yourselves unfading treasures which will render you "Fairest among thousands, altogether lovely."

Sister Marshal, you will now conduct our sisters to their respective stations.

Members of ....Chap. No. ...., in all associations there must be some who rule, and some who obey that rule. The officers whom you have elected to govern this Chapter for the coming year are, I trust, so familiar with the rules of our Order as to be in no danger of exceeding their lawful powers.

The affairs of our Chapter are now in readiness for the work of a new year. We know not what is before us, nor whether a day or a year will be entrusted to us. It behooves us therefore to labor with all diligence, increasing our zeal in the furtherance of the high aims of our Order.

To further the objects of our organization we purpose to give protection to the widow and orphan, to extend comfort when it is needed, to give a ready sympathy to those in sorrow and to offer relief to the poor and needy.

In all our work, and in all our associations, let us be governed by the golden rule "Whatsoever ye would that men should do unto you do ye even so to them." Let us be "kind, one to another, tender hearted, forgiving one another." Let us return good for evil, avoiding all gossip and slander. Only in peace and concord shall we be able to accomplish our purposes, and realize the pure happiness of that companionship which is one of the aims of this organization. So shall we know the truth of the words "Behold how good and how pleasant it is for brethern to dwell together in unity!" So may we confidently hope that in the good providence of God each of us will be brought through a useful and happy life to a blissful close and a triumphant entrance into our celestial home.

Worthy Matron, the officers of your Chapter have been duly installed into their various stations, and are prepared to fulfill their duties during the coming year.

You will now receive into your charge the Charter, by the authority of which this Chapter is held. It must be present at every meeting of the Chapter. You will also receive into your charge the Constitution of the Order in this State, and the By-laws of this Chapter, with both of which you are expected to familiarize yourself, in order to secure enforcement of the rules, regulations and By-laws.

Last of all, I present to you this Gavel, emblem of your authority. Since no one should refuse to obey it, I confidently trust that you will never use it in an arbitrary or dictatorial manner, remembering that justice should be tempered with mercy. You will now assume your station as Worthy Matron of .... Chapter, No. ....

[The Worthy Matron steps to the center of the dais, exchanging places with the Installing Officer. She then gives three blows with the gavel. The Chapter rises. * * *.]

Inst. Officer. Sister Marshal, you will now proclaim the officers of .... Chapter No. .... duly and regularly installed.

M. I hereby, under instruction from the Worthy .... do declare and proclaim the officers of .... Chapter, No. .... duly and regularly installed for the coming year.

[If the Installation Ceremony succeeds the Instituting of a new Chapter, the Worthy Matron on taking her place should suggest that the members give the Grand Honors to the distinguised guests, the Grand Officers.]

INSTALLATION CEREMONIES FOR THE OFFICERS OF A GRAND CHAPTER OR OF THE GENERAL GRAND CHAPTER

The ceremony as given is for use in the Grand Chapter. Only the changes in titles are required to adapt the same ceremony for the installation of officers in the General Grand Chapter. Thus when the Grand Chapter is mentioned, it should be changed to General Grand Chapter; the Grand Matron and Grand Patron should be changed to Most Worthy Grand Matron and Most Worthy Grand Patron; "Right Worthy" should be prefixed to the titles of Associate Grand Matron, Grand Conductress, and Associate Grand Conductress, and "Worthy" before the rest of the Grand titles when used for the General Grand Chapter.

To install the officers of a Grand Chapter a Past Grand Matron or Past Grand Patron should preside, or in their absence a venerable Past Matron may take the chair.

As in the installation of officers, the Grand Marshal collects the insignia of office for use in the ceremonies.

Inst. Officer. The Grand Secretary will call the roll of the newly elected and appointed officers, and the Grand Marshal will arrange them ready to receive the obligation of office.

The Grand Marshal arranges the Grand according to their rank, in a semi-circle around the Altar, facing the Installing Officer.

Gr. Mar. Grand ...., the sisters and brothers now in order before you are the officers newly elected and appointed to conduct the affairs of this Grand Chapter and to perform their regular official duties for the coming year.

Inst. Officer (calling up the Grand Chapter) • • • Members of the Grand Chapter, these officers whom you have chosen are now ready to assume their obligations and duties. They have been chosen because their reputation, their work, and their high moral character inspire our confidence. Do you now desire that they should be installed into the offices for which they have been chosen, promising to support them in the fulfillment of their official duties?

[The members answer in the affirmative.]

Inst. Officer. My Sister and Brothers elect, you have been honored by the members of this Grand Chapter, who have chosen you to represent them in the important work of the Grand

Chapter for the coming year. Yours is not only a great honor, but a great responsibility. You will now take upon yourselves the obligation of office.

Do you, each one, solemnly promise to faithfully and impartially perform the duties of your office; to support the Constitution of this Grand Chapter; to obey its rules, regulations and By-Laws, and to secure obedience to them, striving to be useful and worthy of the trust committed to you?

[After the officers give their assent, the Grand Chapter is seated. * .]

Gr. Mar. Grand ...., I have the honor to present Sister .... for installation as Grand Matron for the coming year.

Inst. Officer. My sister, you have just been given the highest honor in the power of this Grand Chapter to bestow upon a Sister — an honor of which you are justly deserving. Accept my congratulations for your preference.

The high honors of your position carry with them responsibilities requiring careful attention and discrimination. You will be expected to safeguard the interests of this Grand Chapter; to maintain the proper enforcement of its laws and orders throughout its jurisdiction, and to furnish in your own conduct an example of sincere courtesy, fairness, orderliness and respect to law that will inspire the emulation of all of the members of our Order who come under your influence. You will now receive the badge of your office.

Inst. Officer. (Calling up the Grand Chapter * * *.) Members of the Grand Chapter, Order of the Eastern Star, of the State of ...., you see before you your Grand Matron for the coming year. You will indicate your support and confidence by saluting her with the Grand Honors.

Sister ——————, this Grand Chapter salutes you as Grand Matron. You will now be conducted to your station.

[Seats the Grand Chapter. * The Grand Matron is seated in the center of the dais in the East.]

Gr. Mar. Grand ...., I have the honor to present to you for installation Brother ...., Grand Patron elect for the coming year.

Inst. Officer. Brother ...., I congratulate you on the high honor which the members of this Grand Chapter have conferred upon you in electing you to the most important office which they are able to give to a Brother. In so doing your associates have expressed their confidence in your splendid ability, and in your devotion to our Order, knowing that you will gladly accept the responsibilities of your position together with the honors and privileges. You will issue the dispensations, direct the organization and supervision of new Chapters and assist the Grand Matron in her work. Other duties pertaining to your office may be noted by you in the course of your service as Grand Patron. You will now receive the jewel of your office.

Inst. Officer. (Calling up the Grand Chapter * * *.) Members of the Grand Chapter, Order of the Eastern Star, of the State of ...., you see before you your Grand Patron for the coming year. You will salute him with the Grand Honors, thus assuring him of your support and trust.

Brother ...., your brothers and sisters in this Grand Chapter salute you as their Grand Patron. You will now be conducted to your station.

[The Grand Patron is seated at the left of the Grand Matron.]

Gr. M. Grand ...., I have the

pleasure of presenting Sister .... **for** installation as Associate Grand Matron for the coming year.

Inst. Officer. Sister ...., the name of your office indicates your duties. You will assist the Grand Matron, and substitute for her when necessary. The Grand Chapter looks to you to secure faithful adherence to the ritual in our ceremonies. In electing you to this responsible position the members of this Grand Chapter have expressed their faith in your loyalty to our organization. You will now receive the insignia of your office and be conducted to your official station in the West.

Gr. M. Grand ...., I take pleasure in presenting to you for installation Brother ...., Associate Grand Patron elect for the coming year.

Inst. Officer. Brother ...., your election to this high office is a mark of confidence of your associates, and I congratulate you. You will be called upon to assist the Grand Patron, and to substitute for him whenever it is required of you. Perfect familiarity with the rules and principles of our Order will be necessary to enable you to perform your duties creditably and to furnish that excellent example which is due from one of your position and influence.

You will now be invested with the badge of your office, after which you will be conducted to your proper station in the West, at the left of the Associate Grand Matron.

Gr. M. Grand ...., I have the pleasure of presenting to you Brother (or Sister) ...., Grand Secretary elect for the coming year.

Inst. Officer. Brother (or Sister ...., the officer of Grand Secretary is one of the utmost importance, and very difficult to fill. It requires special ability and diligence. You are the link of communication between the officers and the members of this Grand Chapter, and between the Grand Chapter and the Subordinate Chapters. In addition to being the official correspondent for the Grand Chapter, you also represent it financially, having the authority to collect all moneys due it, and recording all accounts and proceedings of the Grand Chapter. You are the keeper of the seal and the records. Your election to this position is a tribute to your high integrity and to your skill, for the success of our Order depends in a large measure upon the faithful discharge of your duties. You will now receive the jewel of your office, and be conducted to your station in the Southeast.

Gr. M. Grand ...., it is my pleasant duty to present Sister ....for installation as Grand Treasurer for the coming year.

Inst. Officer. Sister ...., all the funds of this Chapter will be entrusted to you for you to preserve and pay out as ordered. The Grand Secretary will receive all moneys, record them, and turn them over to you. You will take care of them, paying them out only on the order of this Grand Chapter, keeping a careful record of all receipts and disbursements. If you perform these exacting duties faithfully you will merit the confidence and gratitude of this Grand Chapter.

You will now be invested with the emblem of your office, and conducted to your station in the Northeast.

Gr. M. Grand...........................,, I take pleasure in presenting to you for installation as Grand Conductress Sister ...., and Sister ...., for installation as Associate Grand Conductress, for the coming year.

Inst. Officer. My sisters, you will take an

active part in the work of our Grand Chapter. You will aid the Grand Officers, welcome and introduce visitors, and assist in the performance of our rites and ceremonies. It is within your power to add to the dignity and beauty of these ceremonies by attending to your duties in the proper manner. You will now be invested with the badges appropriate to your offices, and be conducted to your stations, respectively in the South and in the North.

Gr. M. Grand ...., it is an honor to present to you for installation as Grand Chaplain, Brother ...., apointed for the comang year.

Inst. Officer. Brother ...., as Grand Chaplain you will conduct all of the devotional exercises of the Grand Chapter, both in public and in private ceremonies. Our splendid institution is founded upon the great moral precepts of the Bible, and in our work we turn to this Holy Book for inspiration. In all our ways we acknowledge Him who will direct our paths. We must needs seek the Divine approval and aid in doing those good works which are a part of the life of our Order. Through you we shall study His word and seek His guidance. It will be your duty to

direct the charitable and benevolent enterprises of this Grand Chapter, we trust with
such success that the light of this "Eastern
Star" may shine more and more unto the Perfect Day.

You will now be invested with the emblem
of your office, and be conducted to your station
at the right of the Grand Matron.

Gr. M. Grand ...., I have the pleasure
of presenting for installation Brother (or Sister) ...., Grand Lecturer for the coming year.

Inst. Officer. Brother (or Sister) ....,
this Grand Chapter and all of the Subordinate
Chapters within its jurisdiction look to you for
light upon the Rite, the traditions and the
ceremonies of Our Order. You will be expected
to elucidate the meaning of the work; to see
that the ritual is used intelligently and without change; to enlighten the uninformed and
to impress upon all the beauty and high intent
of our noble Order.

You will now be invested with the insignia
of your office, and be conducted to your station
in the South.

Gr. M. Grand ...., I take pleasure
in presenting Sister (or Brother) ....,

for installation as Grand Marshal, for the coming year.

Inst. Officer. Sister (or Brother) ...., you have been honored by appointment to an office requiring great proficiency. Your duty is to arrange all processions of the Grand Chapter; to announce and conduct the officers at the installation, and to render assistance in the ceremonies at all times. You will now be invested with the emblem of your office, and be conducted to your station in the Southeast.

Gr. M. Grand ...., I now present with pleasure Sister ...., for installation as Grand Organist for the coming year.

Inst. Officer. Sister ...., the spell of music woven into the rites and ceremonies of our Order adds to their impressiveness and beauty. Thus it becomes your pleasant duty to contribute to the charm and power of our work. You will now be invested with the jewel of your office, and conducted to your station.

Gr. M. Grand ...., I have the pleasure of presenting Sister .... for installation as Grand Warder for the coming year.

Inst. Officer. Sister ...., you are the inner guard of the Grand Chapter, being stationed just inside the door, where you will announce visitors. You will assure yourself of the right of any strangers to visit the Grand Chapter, thus preventing the intrusion of any improper persons into our secret proceedings.

You will now receive the emblem of your office, and be conducted to your station.

Gr. M. Grand ...., I now have the pleasure of presenting to you for installation the five Sisters who have been chosen to represent the illustrious women whose histories form the inspiration of our Order — — —. Sister ...., as Grand Adah; Sister ...., as Grand Ruth; Sister ...., as Grand Esther; Sister ...., as Grand Martha; Sister ...., as Grand Electa.

Inst. Officer. Sisters, yours is the pleasant duty of personating the noble heroines of our Order. You are to teach their histories during the opening exercises and whenever it is required of you, making the lessons impressive and inspiring to your hearers. It is in your power to further the interests of our organization by discharging your duties in an intelligent and dignified manner.

You will now be invested with the jewels appropriate to your offices, and be conducted to your sations at the five points of our Star.

Gr. M. Grand ...., I now present with pleasure Brother ...., for installation as Grand Sentinel for the coming year.

Inst. Officer. Brother ...., you are the outer guard of the Grand Chapter. Your station is outside the door, where you will be turbances from without. It is an important on guard to prevent any interruptions or dis- post, requiring care and watchfulness to main- tain that secrecy which is necessary in our mystic ceremonies.

You will now be invested with the emblem of your office, and be conducted to your station.

[The Installing Officer calls up the Grand officers. • •]

Inst. Officer. Officers of the Grand Chapter, Order of the Eastern Star, of the State of ...., you are now ready to begin a year of service in the high posts of honor for which you have been chosen by the members of the Grand Chapter. May you fulfill your duties with zeal and devotion, guided by the noble principles of our order, giving gener- ously of your time and your talents in re- turn for the confidence imposed in you.

[The Instlling Officer calls up the Grand Chaper. * * *.]

Inst. Officer. Sisters and Brotners, your Grand Officers for the coming year have been duly elected and installed, and all is in readiness for the work of a new year. You look to these officers with pride and confidence, trusting them to labor zealously for the good of this Grand Chapter and of our beautiful Order. They in turn look to you for hearty support and co-operation. Let us labor together in peace and concord, embodying those high principles of fraternial love and benevolence upon which our organization rests, so that in all of our transactions we shall reflect the light of our glorius Star.

The Grand Marshal will now proclaim the Grand Officers duly elected and installed.

Gr. M. In the name of the Grand Chapter, Order of the Eastern Star, State of ...., and by order of the Grand ...., I do now proclaim the officers of this Grand Chapter duly and regularly elected and installed, being invested with their official badges, and stationed properly for the performance of their duties.

Inst. Officer. We will be led in prayer.

[The Grand Chaplain offers a prayer, after which the Installing Officer seats the Grand Chapter.]

INSTITUTING A NEW CHAPTER.

When a new Chapter of the Order of the Eastern Star is to be established and inaugurated, the ceremony of Instituting should precede the installation of officers. Everything should be made ready as for the regular Installation Ceremonies, with the badges of office collected ready for use, and the new board of officers seated together at one side of the room. As it has been stated before, the first officers of a Chapter must be installed by a Grand Matron, or a Grand Patron, or a Deputy, and the Grand Officer chosen to be the Installing Officer will also preside over the Instituting of the Chapter.

If the Grand Patron is to act as the Presiding Officer, the Grand Matron will ascend the dais, and call the meeting to order, or vice versa. The other Grand Officers will remain in the ante-room, with the exception of the Associate Grand Conductress, who occupies the official chair of the Associate Conductress.

G. M. Sister Associate Grand Conductress, you will invite the Grand Officers to enter the Chapter Room.

[The Associate Grand Conductress throws open the door, and the Grand Officers march in in the regular order (as in the opening exercises). The Grand Patron ascends the dais and the Grand Matron hands him the gavel. The other Grand Officers occupy the stations of the regular officers.]

G. P. The Grand Chapter of the Order of the Eastern Star, in the State of ...., after due deliberation has granted a Charter to the members of this Chapter, extending to them the regular rights and privileges due a Chapter of the Order. The Grand Secretary will now read this Charter. (She does so.)

G. P. Sisters and Brethren, you have heard this Charter read. Do you wish to accept it as you have heard it?

Members. We do.

G. P. (Calling up the Chapter) • • • You will now make your pledges of allegiance to the Order of the Eastern Star, vowing that you will never reveal unlawfully any of the secrets of the Order; that you will obey the Constitution and By-laws, the rules and regulations of the Order; that you will be impartial and conscientious in the selection of new members, never being dominated by personal feelings, but choosing only those candidates who have a perfect right to membership; to do everything within your power to further the interests of the Order, and of this Chapter. If you hereby give your assent to these pledges, you will repeat after me these words: (All repeat after him).

Members. I do solemnly promise that I will, to the best of my ability, keep these reasonable vows.

G. P. Let us pray for God's blessing on our endeavors.

PRAYER.

[By the Grand Chaplain (or Grand Patron)]

Our Father in heaven, Thou hast heard the vows of these Thy servants. Wilt Thou strengthen their hearts to fulfill their pledges; to walk honorably and uprightly as true members of this beloved Order; to so labor that they shall bring upon the Order Thy blessing, doing all to Thine honor and glory. Amen.

Members. So may it be.

G. P. (Seating the Chapter.) * Let us hear the word of God in those lessons which rightly belong to these ceremonies.

Grand Chaplain. I will read the Holy Scriptures appointed for these Ceremonials. Judges 11, 30-36. (He reads) Ruth I; 16-17; II:4, 5. (he reads) Esther V. 1-3 (he reads) John XI, 20-26. (reads) 2 John I, 2-5. (reads).

G. P. Sisters and Brethren, it is an occasion of great happiness when we meet together for the purpose of Instituting a new Chapter of our beloved Order. The Grand Officers congratulate the members of this new Chapter, and rejoice with you, wishing for the Chapter the greatest success and prosperity.

Membership in a Chapter of the Order of the Eastern Star brings many joys and pleasures: the pleasures of congenial companionship; of witnessing and taking part in beautiful ceremonies; of hearing eloquent addresses; of studying great lessons:—the joys of serving ones friends; of relieving distress; of ministering to the sick or needy; of making other people happy. It is a real privilege to be identified with this great company of splendid men and women, united by bonds of faith and trust, of loving service, and high ideals.

As a Chapter you will find many responsibilities falling upon you. To insure the success and honor of your Chapter it will be necessary for each member to strive earnestly and sincerely for the good of the Order. If each member feels responsible for the welfare of the Chapter, then there can be no failures, and there will be no limit to the good which the Chapter will accomplish.

Let your meetings be not mere ceremonies, but let them be characterized by a real interest in the lessons of the Order: a friendly and social spirit: and a genuine desire to labor for the benevolent purposes of the Order.

If the undertakings of the Chapter proceed happily and sincerely, then its influence will extend far beyond the pale of its membership. Its benign force and example will be felt in the whole community, and it will be acclaimed a blessing to society.

(Calls up the Chapter   *   *   *   )

In the name of the Grand Chapter of the State of ...., Order of the Eastern Star, I do now pronounce this Chapter to be duly Instituted as a Chapter of the Order, bearing the name of .... Chapter, No. ...., Order of the Eastern Star, as stated in its Charter. May it here be dedicated to Benevolent enterprises; to the pursuit of the True, the Good, and the Peaceful. May its membership be united in Concord and in Love. May the Chapter reap its full measure of prosperity and success.

Sisters and Brethren, let us sing an Ode

to celebrate the Inaugurating of a new Chapter of our great Order.

[After the singing the Chapter is seated, • and the installation of officers takes place.

It is customary for the Officers of the Grand Chapter to assist in the Dedication of a hall to the work of the Order of the Eastern Star, the Grand Patron presiding, although the services may be conducted by the Subordinate Chapter without assistance.

Such ceremonies are usually public, so that the regular opening ceremonies are dispensed with. If only members are present, the Chapter will be opened in the usual manner.

The hall should be decorated with flowers of the emblematic colors and with the banners of the Order. Special music may be provided and introduced at appropriate times.

When the Grand Officers are in charge of the services, they assemble in the outer room, forming a procession in the usual order. The Worthy Matron takes her place in the East, and the other Chapter officers occupy their regular places, later giving them up to the Grand Officers and taking chairs to the left. The Associate Grand Conductress should carry flowers and a small vessel of oil; the Grand Conductress should carry a vessel containing fruit, also some flowers; the Grand Matron should carry a vessel with salt, also flowers, and the Associate Grand Matron should carry a vessel containing wheat, also some flowers.

The Worthy Matron ascends the dais and calls the Chapter to order.   * .]

W. M.   Sister Warder, will you throw open the door of the Chapter Room for the entrance of the Grand Officers.

[The Grand Officers march in, to music. The Worthy Matron calls up the Chapter   *   *   *   , and invites the Grand Matron and Grand Patron to the East.]

W. M.   Brothers and Sisters, let us salute the Grand Officers with the Grand Honors.

Grand Matron and Grand Patron, and all of the Grand Officers present, we salute you, and heartily bid you welcome.   (Hands the gavel to Grand Patron).

G. P.   Worthy Matron, and members of this Chapter, we thank you for your cordial welcome, and would express our sincere pleasure in joining you on this happy occasion. The Grand Officers will betake themselves to their several stations.

[The Grand Patron calls the Chapter to order.   * .]

W. M.   Grand Patron, as you suggest, this is indeed a happy occasion, when we meet to dedicate this hall to the uses of a Chapter of the Order of the Eastern Star, with all its benevolent and friendly aims. We have invited you to participate in our pleasure, and to conduct these services of dedication.

G. P. Worthy Matron, Sisters and Brothers, we consider it a privilege to have a part in the dedication of this beautiful hall to the noble purposes of our Order. It seems beautiful to us now, and yet this hall will be far more beautiful when it has become hallowed by pleasant memories of earnest service, friendly companionship, and sincere instruction in the splendid principles of our Order. Let us here highly resolve that from this room shall emanate such radiance from our shining Star, that the beneficent light of our Order shall be felt both near and far. Realizing that our aims can never be accomplished without the aid of our heavenly Father, let us unite in seeking His guidance and blessing.

PRAYER.
(By the Grand Chaplain.)

Our heavenly Father, regard the supplication of Thy servants, that this hall, which we here dedicate to service in Thy name, may shelter many who may be renewed in spirit within its walls. May Thy children who meet here to study lessons found in the Holy Scriptures be endued with such seriousness, affection, and devotion of mind, that Thou mayest accept their duty and service, and render unto them the benefits which Thou mayest see fit to give them.

We know that since this hall is to be devoted to good works Thou wilt favorably approve our purpose of setting it apart solemnly and wilt bless our undertakings in it.

Forgive us our shortcomings; inspire us to true nobility of purpose, and the happy realization of our aims. May we meet here as Sisters and Brethren of one Father, rejoicing in good fellowship.

Finally we ask Thee to bless our enterprises with such success as may tend most to Thy glory and the furtherance of our happiness, both temporal and spiritual. Amen.

Response. So may it be.

[Special vocal music may be introduced here, or else an Ode may be sung after which the Grand Officers will rise in turn, and read or repeat the following, or other appropriate selections from the Bible:]

Grand Matron. Psalm xxiv.

Associate Grand Matron. Psalm cxxii.

Grand Conductress. I Kings viii; 27-29.

Associate Grand Conductress. Proverbs ix; 1; xii, 7.

Grand Treasurer. Proverbs 3; 33, and Psalm xxvi; 8.

Grand Secretary. Mark III, 25, and Galatians vi, 10.

Grand Lecturer. Psalm xc, 1, 2; and Psalm xci, 1, 2.

Associate Grand Patron. Psalms lxxxi, 1-3; cxxvii, 1; ci.

G. P. We will now proceed with our services of dedication, with special music.

(If there is no special music, an ode may be sung.)

A. G. C. With this vessel of oil, symbolizing the oil of contentment, and with these flowers, as the flowers of peace, I do now consecrate this hall to Peace. (She points to a banner of Peace which should be hung near her. She advances to the Altar, strewing flowers as she goes, and places the vessel of oil upon it, saying):

A. G. C. Glory be unto God in the highest, and on earth peace, good will to men.

As she returns she says:

A. G. C. Behold, how good and how pleasant it is for brethren to dwell together in unity. In the name of the Father I speak.

G. Cond. With the fruit of abundance, and the flowers of plenty, I consecrate this hall to Charity.

[Points to a banner of Charity, suspended near her. Strewing flowers, she advances to the Altar, and places upon it the dish or basket of fruit, saying:]

G. Cond. May the members of this Chapter never fail to respond to an appeal for Charity. I speak in the name of the heroines of our Order.

[As she returns to her place she says:]

G. Cond. And now abideth faith, hope, charity, these three; but the greatest of these is charity.

Associate Grand Matron. With this grain, like good seed, and these flowers here sown, I consecrate this hall to Truth.

[She points to the banner of Truth which should be hung near her. Then, approaching the Altar, while strewing flowers, she places the vessel of grain on the Altar, saying:]

A. G. M. As the seed is sown in the ground, and the flowers are planted, and spring forth in abundance, so Truth, crushed to earth, shall rise again. I speak in the name of the Grand Chapter.

[As she returns to her place, she says:]

A. G. M. I have chosen the way of truth: Thy jugments have I laid before me.

G. Matron. With this salt, as an emblem of hospitality, and these flowers typifying the Divine wisdom, I here consecrate this hall to Wisdom. (Pointing to a banner of Wisdom, near her.) May all who enter here feel the warmth of hospitality, and learn from words of Wisdom. In the name of the Order of the Eastern Star, I speak.

[As she speaks she advances to the Altar, strewing flowers, and placing the vessel of salt on the Altar. As she returns to her station, she says:]

G. M. Be kindly affectioned, one to another with brotherly love; in honor preferring one another; not slothful in business; fervent in spirit; serving the Lord; rejoicing in hope; patient in tribulation; continuing instant in prayer; distributing to the necessity of saints; given to hospitality.

G. P. In the name of Faith, of Hope, of Charity, of Love, and of Virtue; in the name of the teachings of our Order, of devotion to principles·of right; of constancy in religious devotion; of faithfulness to kindred and friends; of unswerving faith in the time of trouble; of patient submission to wrongs; I do now dedicate this Hall to the uses of the Order of the Eastern Star. May the light of our Star shine forth more and more unto the perfect day, cheering and comforting and inspiring with its benign rays, lighting the way unto that house eternal, not builded with hands.

The Grand Marshal will now promulgate the dedication of this hall.

G. M. By order of the Grant Patron of the Grand Chapter of the State of........, Order of the Eastern Star, I officially announce that this hall has been regularly dedicated to the uses of the Order, under the auspices of...... Chapter, No..........

[If any special speakers have been secured for this occasion, their addresses may follow, also any special music or other program of entertainment.]

ADMINISTRATIVE DEGREE FOR THE WORTHY MATRON OF A CHAPTER OF THE ORDER OF THE EASTERN STAR.

The Administrative Degree is conferred upon a Worthy Matron-elect just before her installation, or as soon thereafter as possible. It is strictly an official degree and is designed to explain clearly to the Worthy Matron her responsibilities, obligations and powers, and to unite those who have the governing power in the Order by an understanding sympathy and spirit of helpfulness.

The degree is conferred in the Chapter Room by the Administrative Council, consisting of three or more Worthy Patrons, Past Worthy Patrons, Worthy Matrons, Past Worthy Matrons, and any officers of the Grand Chapter of the State, or of the General Grand Chapter. The Worshipful Masters, Past Worshipful Masters, and Officers of the Grand Lodge of the Masonic fraternity may also be present, and take part in the work of the degree.

The meeting is called by the Worthy Patron or by a Grand Officer of the State in which the Chapter is located. If the degree is conferred before the installation of officers, the retiring Worthy

Patron presides; if after the installation, the newly installed Worthy Patron may preside. A Sentinel is appointed to guard the door. After the officers have assembled the meeting is called to order by the Worthy Patron presiding. *

W. P. Sister- and Brother-officers, we have met together to celebrate the election of Sister .... to the distinguished office of Worthy Matron of ...., Chapter No. ...., of the Order of the Eastern Star, by conferring upon her the honorary Administrative Degree. It is eminently proper that one who, by her superior gifts, has attained to this high position, should receive due recognition of the honor from her fellow officers. It is also justly due her from those who have filled such positions as hers and have gained a rich experience, that they should instruct her in the requirements and responsibilities of her office.

Before proceeding further, let us invoke the Divine blessing.

[One of the officers is called upon to offer prayer. The Chapter is called up. * * *]

PRAYER.

(By the Chaplain, or one of the Officers.)

Almighty God, we bow before Thee, seeking

Thy blessing upon this company. Although we may all have attained to some measure of earthly honor, we are humble before Thee, knowing that we are but poor creatures in Thy sight. Guide us as we struggle on in the upward journey, and bless us in our worthy enterprises. Let Thine especial blessing fall upon this sister; endow her with wisdom and judgment that she may fulfill her obligations worthily in Thy sight, and that our Star may radiantly reflect Thy honor and glory. Amen.

Response. So may it be.

W. P. (*To the Worthy Matron-elect, who rises as he addresses her.*) Sister ...., in conferring upon you this degree, it is intended to explain and dignify the duties and powers which devolve upon the Matron of a Chapter of the Order of the Eastern Star. To illustrate some of the qualities requisite in the presiding officer of a Chapter of our Order, the story of Deborah has been chosen, as given in the Holy Scriptures. Sister ...., Past Worthy Matron (or a Grand Matron) will give the history for this degree, as depicted in the story of Deborah.

Past W. M. Sister ...., I congratulate you on your election to this most important post. It is a pleasure to impart to you some of the traditional knowledge of this degree. In the storied past, in that time over three thousand years ago, when Israel was ruled by Judges, there dwelt in the land a prophetess by the name of Deborah. Between Ramah and Bethel, on Mount Ephraim she and her husband Lapidoth lived in a tent under a palm tree. The people of Israel had done evil in the sight of the Lord, and He had sold them into bondage, to Jabin, King of Canaan, who reigned in Hazor, the captain of whose army was Sisera. For twenty years he mightily oppressed the children of Israel, and they cried unto the Lord.

Now Deborah was a woman of great wisdom, and she judged Israel at that time. For her counsel and judgment the Israelites came up to Ephraim where she dwelt under the palm tree. The great oppression and sorrows of her countrymen grieved her. She answered the appeal of the people to try to effect their deliverance as a "Mother in Israel". She rose up, and sought for a leader to carry the Israelites to victorious battle.

Barak, the son of Abinoam, who dwelt in Kedesh of Naphtali, was the man to whom she revealed her plan. She called him to her and explained to him the plan which had been given to her as the will of God. She told him that he should take ten thousand warriors of Naphtali and Zebulun and go up to Mount Tabor. She would attract Sisera, the Captain of King Jabin's army, to the river Kishon, where the multitude of his hosts, and his nine hundred chariots of iron should be delivered into the hand of Barak.

Barak answered: "If thou wilt go with me, then will I go: but if thou wilt not go with me, then will I not go." For he was impressed by the vast multitude opposing him. Yet he felt that Deborah, with her courage and God-given wisdom could help him to victory. Deborah answered him: "I will surely go with thee: notwithstanding the journey that thou takest shall not be for thine honour: for the Lord shall sell Sisera into the hand of a woman". And Deborah arose and went with Barak to Kedesh.

Then Barak gathered at Kedesh ten thousand men of Naphtali and Zebulun, and he went up to Mount Tabor with the army; and Deborah went also, as she had promised.

Sisera heard that the army of Israel had

gone up into Mount Tabor, and he gathered his forces unto the river Kishon. Nine hundred chariots of iron he brought, and a great multitude of his skilled warriors. The downtrodden Israelites were sorely in need of encouragement, to enable them to make the attempt to conquer such a host. Deborah gave them the needed inspiration, crying to Barak: "Up: for this is the. day in which the Lord hath delivered Sisera into thine hand: is not the Lord gone out before thee?"

So Barak took his army of ten thousand and went down from Mount Tabor. There the Lord discomfited Sisera and all his chariots and all his hosts with the edge of the sword before Barak. Barak and his men pursued after the chariots and after the hosts of Sisera, and every man of Sisera's army was felled, and there was not a man left. Sisera jumped down from his chariot and ran away on foot. He stopped at the tent of Heber the Kenite, for rest and food, and while he slept he was slain by the hand of a woman, as Deborah had prophesied.

Then the Israelites rejoiced and sang songs of praise. Deborah and Barak also rejoiced with them, but they did not take the credit or the glory of the victory. They sang: "Praise ye the Lord for the avenging of Israel, when the people freely offered themselves. I will sing praise unto the Lord: I will sing praise unto the God of Israel."

And the land had rest forty years.

From the example of this illustrious woman we may see what one woman may do for a whole nation by inspiring in them a strong faith and courage.

P. W. P. The signs and passes of this degree are taken from the history just related. Do you promise to preserve any secrets which may now be divulged to you?

W. M. I do.

P. W. P. When Deborah wished to speak to Barak, she called him from his home at Kedesh-Naphtali. We use the Sign of the Signal, or the Summons, as a sign of this degree. The response is: "I will surely go with thee" which is the response of Deborah to Barak's request. The Sign of Refusal is also adopted in this degree. Significant words for the degree are those used in the command of Deborah: "Up; for this is the day."

•

[The Charge to the Worthy Matron should now

be delivered by a Grand Officer, a Past Worthy
Matron, or Past Worthy Patron, or by the presiding officer.]

Sister ...., as Deborah in the days of
old inspired her people to faith and action, so
may woman in these modern times wield her
powerful influence. Although she may not
have spectacular powers such as the ability to
prophesy, she may yet accomplish many good
works through her own special gifts. For not
all are blessed with the same talents: our
talents differ according to the grace that is
in us, whether to prophesy; to minister; to
teach; to advise; to give; to rule, or to show
mercy. To one is given wisdom; to another
faith; to another knowledge; to another a
gifted tongue; to another the power of heal-
ing.

Your Chapter in choosing you to preside
over them as Worthy Matron displayed a confidence in your possession of those special
gifts which are most needed to fill that important position: the gift of knowledge, to instruct them wisely; the gift of judgment, to
make just decisions; the gift of eloquence, to
address the Chapter on the many topics coming before it for considerations; the gift of

keen perception, to preserve peace and concord tactfully; and the gift of self-possession, which is indispensable if one would rule others. Invested with these gifts a sister will govern her Chapter with honor to herself and to the name of the Order.

These talents which God hath generously bestowed upon you carry with them serious obligations. For whom he endows so richly, he gives also a work to do and a service to perform which will exercise those talents. One so favored has a certain responsibility toward those who have not been so fortunate. She is a leader who should direct others, as Deborah directed the children of Israel, working for the best interests of her people.

Your first duty is to your own Chapter, to govern it well, to inspire in the members such an interest, such zeal and devotion to the work of the Chapter as will reflect credit upon the entire Order. Our beautiful Star must not shine for us alone, however, for its rays should penetrate into the darkness of the world, bringing light and joy and happiness, so that the light of the Star may benefit those both near and far. In so doing may your most onerous duties be a joy to you, and may the members of the Chapter unite in calling you blessed. You may expect the support of your associates in the Chapter, and of the officers of the Order, who make the promise " I will surely go with thee".

With the story of Deborah still in mind, I charge you to enter bravely upon your duties. "Up; for this is the day."

We will now be dismissed with a benediction, after which the Chapter will be closed for a social hour.

BENEDICTION.

(By one of the officers).

Lord, dismiss us with Thy blessing. Pity our weaknesses, encourage our best efforts, and finally unite us with Thee in the joy of heaven. Amen.

Response. So may it be.

P. W. P. I now declare the Chapter closed. •

THE COMPLIMENTARY DEGREE OF QUEEN OF THE SOUTH.

This is an honorary degree to be conferred upon all active members of a Chapter of the Order of the Eastern Star who are considered worthy of this distinction. All of those members who have received this degree may be present, and the officers of the Chapter will take their places. The group, instead of bearing the name of a Chapter, is known as a Palace, and the regular officers receive the following titles for this degree only:

Worthy Patron, KING SOLOMON.
Worthy Matron, QUEEN BATHSHEBA.
Associate Matron, PRINCESS HATTIPHA.
Conductress, PRINCESS OZIEL.
Associate Conductress, PRINCESS ZORAH.
Treasurer, MYRA.
Secretary, LEAH.
CHAPLAIN, (retaining regular title).
WARDER, (retaining regular title).
SENTINEL, (retaining regular title).
ORGANIST.

The Star officers instead of their regular positions on the points of the Star, occupy places in front of King Solomon, facing him: on his right,

Ruth and Electa: on his left Adah; Esther on the right of Princess Hattipha, in front; Martha, on the left of Princess Hattipha, in front. They are known in this degree by the following titles:

Adah, PRINCESS HAGAR.

Ruth, PRINCESS ORPAH.

Esther, PRINCESS SYENE.

Martha, PRINCESS THARAH.

Electa, PRINCESS ELLAH.

This degree is usually followed by a social hour, banquet or other suitable entertainment. Practically the same preliminaries are observed as in the regular opening ceremonies of the Order, except that the wording is changed to correspond with the requirements of the "Palace" and the officers all take their places before the meeting begins. King Solomon calls the Palace to order in the usual manner (*) and says:

King S. Sister Warder, you will see that the doors to the Palace are secure.

War. Most Excellent King Solomon, the Palace doors are secure.

King S. Sisters and Brethren of the Palace, and Guests within the audience chamber, the hour has arrived for our deliberations, in which I require your attention and assistance. Princess Hattipha, you will ascertain whether all present are entitled to their places in this assembly.

[Princess Hattipha will respond at once, or if she is uncertain, she will call upon Princess Oziel and Princess Zorah to ascertain whether all within the room are entitled to be present.]

Hattipha. Most Excellent King Solomon, I find that all in this assembly are entitled to be present.

King S. It is well. Sister Warder, you will convey this message to the Sentinel: that he shall guard this Palace with vigilance, and prevent any interruptions of our deliberations.

[The Warder communicates with the Sentinel in the usual manner (—— —— — —) and after receiving his response, delivers the message to him.]

War. Most Excellent King Solomon, your message to the Sentinel has been delivered.

[King Solomon calls up the officers, who remain standing during the opening ceremonies. * *]

King S. Princess Hattipha, who are the officers of the Palace, and where are they stationed?

Hattipha. Most Excellent King Solomon, the officers of the Palace are seventeen in number. Their titles and stations are: King Solomon, in the East; Queen Bathsheba, in the

East, on the right of King Solomon; Princess Hattipha, in the West; Princess Oziel, in the South; Princess Zorah, in the North; Myra, in the Northeast; Leah, in the Southeast; Princess Hagar, on the left of King Solomon, in front; Princess Orpah, on the right of King Solomon, in front; Princess Syene, on the right of Princess Hattipha, in front; Princess Tharah, on the left of Princess Hattipha, in front; Princess Ellah, on the right of King Solomon, in front; Warder, at the door, inside, Sentinel, at the door, outside; Marshal, to the right of Leah, in front; Chaplain, to the left of Myra, in front; the Organist seated at the organ.

King S. Queen Bathsheba, enumerate the duties of your station.

Bathsheba. Most Excellent King Solomon, my duties are to intercede in behalf of the Queen of Sheba, and so secure for her the bestowal of your royal favor.

King S. Princess Hattipha, what are your duties in the Palace?

Hattipha. Most Excellent King Solomon, it is my duty to assist in welcoming the Queen of Sheba, and to intercede in her behalf for the gift of your royal favor

King S. Princess Oziel, what are your duties in the Palace?

Oziel. My duties are to see that the Palace is ready for the proper reception of visitors; to receive the Queen of the South and introduce her to the Most Excellent King Solomon.

King S. Princess Zorah, what are your duties in the Palace?

Zorah. My duties are to see that the Palace is in readiness for the proper reception of visitors; to assist Princess Oziel in receiving and introducing the Queen of the South to the Most Excellent King Solomon.

King S. Sister Myra, recount the duties of your station.

Myra. My duties are to receive and deposit all gifts and offerings in the royal treasury of the Most Excellent King Solomon.

King S. Sister Leah, specify the duties of your station.

Leah. Most Excellent King Solomon, my duties are to make the record of the deliberations in the Palace, and preserve them in the chronicles of the kingdom.

King S. This is the true relation of the duties of the Palace. That they may be performed with wisdom and despatch, lot us invoke the Divine counsel.

[Calls up the Chapter. * * *]

PRAYER.

(By the Chaplain.)

Oh Thou Most High and Holy One, Father of All, we bow before Thee in humble supplication. Bless our undertakings we pray Thee. Incline our hearts to keep Thy law, and preserve us from all unrighteousness. Help us to work together in love, in honor preferring one another. May we be upheld by unfailing trust in Thee, knowing that all things work together for good to them that love Thee.

Forgive us our sins, and deliver us from evil, finally uniting us with Thyself in all the blessed company of the angels. Amen.

Response. So may it be.

King S. Sisters and Brethren, there are in the Scriptures, both in the New and the Old Testaments, many stirring incidents, and inspiring accounts of noble characters. Some of the histories have been incorporated into the Degrees of the Order of the Eastern Star. We are all familiar with the stories of those five illustrious heroines upon whose histories are based the five degrees of this Order.

The incident concerning the Queen of Sheba is another one of this class, upon which a degree is founded. Since there are worthy applicants waiting to receive the light and benefits of this degree, I now declare this Palace open for the conferring of the degree. Sister Warder, you will now instruct the Sentinel that we are about to confer the degree of the Queen of the South, and that there must be no interruptions nor alarms from without during this ceremony.

War. Most Excellent King Solomon, your instructions have been obeyed.

King S. The degree of Queen of the South is based upon the story of the visit of the Queen of Sheba to King Solomon, as related in the Holy Scriptures. The name of Solomon has come down to us as a synonym for wisdom, honor and wealth. Even in his own time, when there was no recourse to newspapers, or to any printed word; to the telephone, the telegraph, or wireless communication; when travel was a laborious process by caravan or sailing ship; even then the fame of King Solomon had spread throughout the civilized world. The magnificent temple, and the Royal Palace which he had built; the fabulous riches which he had accumulated; the remarkable wisdom which the king displayed in ruling his subjects and in deciding all questions, gave him a renown which extended to the far corners of what was then known as the world.

Solomon, on ascending the throne to which he succeeded his father David, prayed for an understanding heart, so that he could judge his people and rule them wisely. His prayer was answered, and he was endowed with a wisdom and understanding such as made all people marvel. Riches and honor came to him, and he was indeed a mighty king.

There came to the Palace representatives of all peoples to hear the wisdom of Solomon, from all the kingdoms of the earth, where the fame of his wisdom had spread. All the earth sought Solomon, to hear his wisdom which God had put into his heart.

Among the many famous people who came to visit the king, to prove his knowledge and to profit by his understanding, was the Queen of Sheba. The degree of Queen of the South commemorates this visit.

King Solomon had builded for himself a magnificent Royal Palace, and to this Palace came kings and ambassadors and people of all nations. Seated upon his majestic throne of ivory overlaid with pure gold, and surrounded by his officers and courtiers, King Solomon received all people wisely and graciously.

Princess Zorah, you will retire and ascertain whether any are in waiting to be received into the audience chamber of the Palace.

Zorah. Most Excellent King Solomon, there are certain ladies, relatives of those brethren whom we call Master Masons, and members of the Order of the Eastern Star, who await the royal summons into the Palace. (If there are any men candidates, she adds: "These are accompanied by certain brethren known as Master Masons.") They come seeking entrance into the Palace, that they may hear the words of wisdom which were spoken of old by King Solomon to the Queen of Sheba. They are ready to pledge strict observance of all the rules and regulations of this degree, and are altogether worthy to be admitted into your presence.

King S. Princess Zorah, you will retire to the outer Portals of the Palace, and make ready the candidates for entrance.

[Zorah retires in the usual manner, and prepares the candidates. It is intended that only one candidate should receive the degree at a time. She should represent the Queen of Sheba, and should wear white, with a crown and veil. If there are other women candidates, they and any men candidates may constitute the retinue of the Queen, who is represented by a chosen candidate. . . . . All being ready, Zorah raps on the door —— —— — —, and is answered by Princess Oziel, who opens the door.]

Zorah. Princess Oziel, I bring to the door of the audience chamber, the Queen of Sheba, who is ready and waiting for entrance into the presence of King Solomon.

Oziel. Most Excellent King Solomon, Princess Zorah reports that the Queen of Sheba is ready and waiting for entrance into the audience chamber of the Palace.

King S. Princess Oziel, you will proceed with a suitable escort to welcome and conduct the Queen of Sheba into the presence of the king.

[Music should be played during the entrance of the candidates, who should be attended by Zorah, Oziel, Hagar, Orpah, Syene, Tharah, and Ellah. King Solomon calls up the Chapter. * * *]

Oziel. Most Excellent King Solomon, the noble Queen of Sheba with her retinue stands before you, presenting her written petition, which I bear in my hands.

King S. Let the petition be read by Leah.

Leah. "Sheba, Queen of the South, has heard of the fame of the mighty and illustrious King Solomon, and has come to prove his wisdom with hard questions at Jerusalem. She brings with her a large retinue, and many camels laden with spices, pure gold, and precious stones. She seeks the favor of the king, that he may grant her an audience in his mighty presence."

King S. The request of the most eminent Queen of Sheba has been granted. Let her voice be heard in the royal audience chamber.

Princess Hattipha. Most Excellent King Solomon, I present for your royal favor the most noble and eminent Sheba, Queen of the South.

King S. Mighty Queen, we salute you and welcome you to the royal audience chamber. Be seated. (Seats the Chapter. *) Let the petitions of the most noble Queen be heard.

Hagar. Most Excellent King Solomon, may I be permitted to speak as a proxy for the most noble, the Queen of Sheba?

King S. Speak, Princess Hagar.

Hagar. From a kingdom far to the south, Oh, King, the Queen of Sheba has come to seek thy presence. She has heard of thine illustrious wisdom and honor and riches, and desires to prove thee with hard questions. To the farthest corners of the world thy renown has penetrated. From the ends of the earth they come to learn wisdom from thy lips. From a far country, by a long journey over mountains and rivers and plains has this Queen come up from the South, that she, too, might profit by thy great understanding. A woman, ruler over many people, she seeks wisdom from thy lips, the like of which is not known to other men. As the Most High God hath granted thee a largeness of heart even as the sands of the seashore, may it please thee to hear her petition and to refuse nothing of her request.

King S. Princess Hagar, thou hast spoken well. Most noble Queen of Sheba, commendable is thy zeal and praiseworthy thy earnestness in making the long journey from the South in order to increase thine own wisdom to rule over thy people. Yet am I constrained to refuse thy request. For in the Holy Scriptures, wherein are recorded the dealings of the

Most High God with mankind, there is not to be found any instance where a woman entered into His counsels.

Orpah. Most Excellent King Solomon, hear me for this most eminent Queen, and consider my request.

King S. Speak, Princess Orpah.

Orpah. When David thy royal father was old and stricken in years, men of his kingdom conspired to make thy elder brother Adonijah king. It was then that thy noble mother, Bathsheba went unto the king as he sat in his chamber, a very old man, and warned him of the dangers of the times. She it was who pleaded that thou shouldst not fail to inherit the kingdom and to sit upon the throne as it was promised thee. Thus did thy Mother seek an audience with King David, and secure for thee the throne of Israel. Thus did a woman most surely enter into the purposes and counsels of the Almighty.

At another time, two women, Hebrew mothers, stood up in thy audience chamber and made their claims—each for the one living child, neither for the child that was dead. Through the claims of these two women thou wast called upon to show that wisdom of God

which was in you, to rule and to judge. As
thou didst hearken unto those Hebrew women
and didst prove thy exceeding great wisdom,
so do thou hearken unto me and refuse me not
in my request for the Queen of Sheba.

King S. Princess Orpah, by your reasonable
speech you have overcome the objection which
I offered. Yet in all history I am not able to
find a record of such a request made by a
woman, or of such an audience granted to a
woman. As the King of Israel, I hesitate to
set a precedent in this matter for which I can
find no justification in all the annals of our
history.

Syene. Most Excellent King Solomon, permit me also to speak in behalf of this gracious
Queen.

King S. Speak, Princess Syene.

Syene. Recorded in the Holy Scriptures we
have found instances where the Almighty God
has used the voice of women to proclaim his
decrees. In addition to those illustrious
women named by Princess Orpah, allow me to
remind you of Jael, the wife of Heber, the
Kenite, who by her cleverness and bravery rid
her country forever of its most da gerous
enemy; of Miriam the prophetess, sister of

Moses, whom she was able to aid by her
counsel and praise, while he was the law-giver
and director of the people of Israel; o'
Deborah, another prophetess, dwelling under a
palm tree and judging Israel. She advised
Barak and went with him to counsel him in the
defense of the nation, to save the people from
destruction. In the Holy Writ are so many
examples of women serving as an agent to
work the will of God that surely the wisest of
all rulers will not fail to recognize the worth
of woman, and to acknowledge her claims.
Hear Oh King, my petitions, and grant the
request of this noble Queen.

King S. You have spoken well, Oh Princess
Syene. Yet one other objection presents
itself: the unfortunate reputation of your sex
for indiscretion in talking. The knowledge
which the noble Queen of Sheba seeks to
obtain was communicated to me secretly by
the Most High, in the silent watches of the
night, even as Samuel heard the bidding of
Jehovah in the midnight stillness of the
tabernacle. Would it be becoming in a King
to reveal these secrets to women, to be repeated here and there without reserve? No,
secrets are not to be entrusted to women.

Tharah. Most Excellent King Solomon, allow me to add my voice to the petitions for the Queen of the South.

King S. Proceed, Princess Tharah.

Tharah. Recall, Oh King, the silence of Jochebed, the mother of Moses, in guarding the secret of his birth for three months, braving the anger of Pharaoh, and saving for Israel the nation's greatest counsellor and law-giver. Know, Oh King, that woman is capable of rising to her responsibilities. She has ever been faithful to her trusts. Trust her as a slave, and she may prove to be as unreliable as a slave. Trust her as an equal, and a friend, and her loyalty and firmness will prove her to be in truth an equal and a friend. Surely Oh mighty King, thy noble officers and courtiers can testify to the truth of this claim, from the recollections of wise and helpful mothers, wives, sisters and daughters. If there be in your heart any such memories, hear our petitions, and grant the request of the most eminent Queen of Sheba.

King S. Well have you spoken, Princess Tharah. Yet through the ages woman has been called the inferior of man. Why should the knowledge imparted to man alone be communicated to the weaker creature?

Ellah. Most Excellent King Solomon, permit me to make a further plea in behalf of the Queen of Sheba.

King S. Speak, Princess Ellah.

Ellah. How can it be said that woman is less than man in mind and in soul? She is his helpmeet in sorrow, in trouble and affliction. God's words are spoken to woman as well as to man. This woman before you has been chosen to rule over a mighty people. Since her position is high, and her power is great, should she not be permitted to receive the Divine wisdom necessary for the discharge of her obligations as Queen?

King S. Princess Ellah, your plea is well made. Yet how shall it be said that woman and man shall together receive these secrets, and comply with the requirements of convention, preserving that reserve, modesty and decorous conduct which should attend their associations?

Hattipha. Hear me, Oh King, as I make reply for the Queen of Sheba.

King S. Speak, Princess Hattipha.

Hattipha. You see before you the Queen of Sheba, a woman crowned with royalty and endowed with power to rule over many men. If she be allowed to govern men, why should she not also receive the knowledge to guide her in her judgment? Where is there a question of propriety in filling nobly the station in which God has placed her? But if King Solomon must refuse to divulge the wisdom which he has received from above, then must the Queen of the South return to her home by the long journey over the plains, the rivers and the mountains. To all men must she make reply that the greatest of all rulers, known of all the world for his understanding, has denied her pleas for a share of that Divine wisdom which she urgently required and humbly sought. No more shall her petitions be heard. Blindly will she struggle for some measure of that wisdom which was vouchsafed only to King Solomon. Let her go.

King S. Sister Leah, look you in the Holy Book, in the law and in the prophets, and ascertain whether it will reveal any light on the relation of man and woman.

Leah. Most Excellent King Solomon, all the Scriptures point to the worth of woman in the Divine plan: how that male and female both were created in the image of God: how

that woman was made as a helpmeet for man;
how that the widow is named as an object of
kindly benevolence and affection. The his-
torical books of the Bible name many
illustrious women who took a great part in the
history of Israel. They are always mentioned
in terms of reverence and respect. In God's
favor and mercy these eminent women took
an equal part with man; Samson's mother,
Samuel's mother, those lovely heroines, Ruth,
Esther, Martha, and Jephthah's daughter,
and many other great women of history testify
to the importance of woman in the Divine
purposes.

King S. Tell me, Bathsheba, Mother and
Queen, whether in the writings of my father,
David the King, may be found aught concern-
ing the relations of man and woman.

Bathsheba. In the Psalms of David, your
noble father, Most Excellent King Solomon,
may be found respectful references to woman,
and there is no indication that she is regarded
as an inferior being. In depicting the glories
of the Kingdom of Christ he refers to them
as to a beautiful and virtuous woman. He
speaks of the loss of a mother as the deepest
sorrow that can come to man. In the Psalms

the term man is used as meaning the human race, not as a superior part of that race. As a mother and as a queen I adjure thee, let not thy wisdom be brought into question by a refusal to hear this woman, who has come from afar to prove it.

King S. Righteous lips are the delight of kings. Most noble Sheba, Queen of the South, I must acknowledge that these pleadings have convinced me of the worth of your claims. Although Samson suffered for giving up his secret to Delilah, and Saul fell a victim to the spell of the Witch of Endor, yet have I faith in the sincerity of your motives in seeking the secrets which have been revealed to me. Truly these women thy friends and advocates have spoken with wisdom, and in their tongues is the law of kindness. Adorned with strength and honor is this company of noble women. According to the Holy Scriptures, Jehovah shall lay up sound wisdom for the righteous, and his secrets shall be revealed to them that fear Him.

Sheba. Most Excellent King Solomon, what you have said is wise and good, and upon my return to that far country from whence I came I shall endeavor to pass on these words of wisdom, teaching others what is that good and acceptable thing which the Lord requireth of all who truly love Him. Oh King, gracious Queen Bathsheba, and noble Princesses who have spoken for me, permit me to thank you for your faith in womankind here so confidently expressed. Never shall you have reason to regret this confidence, nor may the King fear that any woman shall unlawfully reveal the secrets entrusted to her.

[King Solomon seats all and calls the Palace to order * .]

King S. Sisters and Brethren, by means of this beautiful allegory we have regarded the various objections that have been presented against the admission of women into a knowledge of the principles of Freemasonry. The arguments made to King Solomon convinced him of the right of the Queen of Sheba to hear his secrets. In those days prejudice prevented woman from entering into the privileges which she enjoys today. In this enlightened time when woman occupies a place of equal honor with man, in education, in business, in the professions. and in affairs of government, there can be no serious objection to their adoption into Masonry. The honorable and exalted purposes had in view in the dissemination of the knowledge of Masonic principles can have no opposition worthy of the name. Its effects in winning to the advocacy of Masonry the virtuous, intelligent and influential women members of the families of Masons are truly encouraging, and stimulate its friends to persevere in the general promulgation of the system. According to the tenets of the Order of the Eastern Star, Adoptive Masonry stands a bright monument to feminine secrecy and fidelity, and proves the error of those who fancy a woman is not to be trusted with a secret. There is not in the whole of the ceremonies of this Rite a single point with which the most ascetic moralist could find fault. On the contrary, all is pure, and beautiful; it is among the brighest jewels which adorn the records of Masonry

With the greatest pleasure I hail each woman here as a Queen of the South, with whom Master Masons delight to share Masonic privileges and employments as much as is lawfully permitted.

Bathsheba. The basic secrets of Freemasonry we do not seek to learn. We do not wish to make unreasonable demands upon our

fathers, brothers, or husbands as Master Ma
sons. Yet when we are told that we are intimately bound to the Masonic fraternity by
ties most tender and lasting, we seek some
tokens of recognition whereby we may know
Masons and be known of them as sharing in
the Masonic privileges. Whatever knowledge
is of advantage to us for the advancement of
womankind, that we desire to know, and Masons will find us worthy of the trust reposed
in us. For "woman's heart beats responsive
to the same inspiration that prompts man to
noble deeds."

King S. Sisters and Brothers, candidates
for the degree of Queen of the South, the purposes of the degree have been so clearly expressed through this dramatic presentation
that further elucidation is unnecessary. As-
suredly there can be no controversy over the
admission of the mothers, wives, daughters
and sisters of Master Masons into the privileges of the Order of the Eastern Star, and
any woman who can prove her claim to those
privileges will be graciously received into the
Order.

Queen Bathsheba, are you aware of any
further deliberations to be held in the Palace

at this time?

Bathsheba. No, Most Excellent King Solomon, there is nothing further, within my knowledge.

King S. Sister Warder, you will inform the Sentinel that we are about to close the Palace, and direct him to permit no interruptions.

[The Warder does so in the usual manner — — — — — —.]

War. Most Excellent King Solomon, your instructions have been obeyed.

King S. Let us sing an Ode before leaving the audience chamber of the Palace.

[Calls up the Palace. * * *]

King S. I now declare this Palace closed. Sister Warder, you will so inform the Sentinel.

[Closes the Palace with one gavel blow. *]

BURIAL SERVICES.

It is customary for the Chapter conducting these services to send a five-pointed star, made of flowers of the emblematic colors of the Order. The members assemble and stand about the grave:— the Marshal, Matron, Patron and Chaplain at the head of the grave, with the other officers back of them, excepting the Star officers and the Associate Matron, who stand three on each side of the grave. The mourners take their places at the foot, and the members of the Chapter form a circle around all. Each of the Star officers should carry a few flowers of the appropriate color, and the Worthy Matron and Worthy Patron should each carry a few flowers for the ceremony.

When all have assembled as above (usually music is played or sung while they are gathering) the Worthy Matron will begin the services, or she may request the Worthy Patron to conduct the ceremonies.

W. M. Sisters and Brethren, in this thoughtful hour we have met together to tender our offerings of respect and love for our departed sister, and to reveal our sympathy for those to whom she was nearest and dearest. In the midst of our sorrow we are confronted with

serions thoughts. We reflect that this dear
sister but yesterday was one of us, and today
is gone, leaving this beautiful world of ours
for that "building of God, a house not made
with hands, eternal in the heavens." She has
passed beyond the influence of earthly praise
or blame. She is ready for that Divine summons, "Come ye blessed of my Father, receive the kingdom prepared for you from the
beginning of the world."

Our sister walked among us in constancy
and with courage, and in departing she has
left a tender memory of her virtues and loveliness. She has finished her course in faith,
and she has laid hold on eternal life. Before
our Altar she studied with us the high principles of our order, and "hast professed a good
profession before many witnesses." In her
life she exemplified the noble virtues taught in
our Order.

She was true to her convictions of right,
faithful to her duty, constant and loyal to
friends and family, hopeful and trusting, in
time of trouble, and always charitable and
truthful. Having served God with constancy
on earth she will be united hereafter with the
blessed company of His saints.

We mourn her loss, and we sorrow with her loved ones. Yet we are not sorry as persons without hope, for we know that an entrance shall be ministered unto us into the everlasting kingdom, where we shall meet and rejoice together.

My friends, as we stand in this solemn presence, we are moved to earnest reflections. Our years are brought to an end as it were a tale that is told. We know not when our summons may come to join that heavenly throng. Let us then consider the words of the apostle: "Therefore my beloved brethren, be ye steadfast, unmoveable, always abounding in the work of the Lord, forasmuch as ye know that your labor is not in vain in the Lord."

Let us sing together a hymn in memory of this dear sister who was wont to sing our Odes with us before our Altar.

[A verse of any suitable hymn may be sung here.]

W. M. The symbols of our Order have a special message for us at this time. These flowers which we bring in loving memory of our sister are symbolic in our Order, of virtues which should beautify our lives. They remind us of the lessons which we, in company with this sister, have often heard from the various points of our Star. It is fitting then that these voices and these lessons should be heard in the final rites for our beloved sister. Let us hear the voices and the tributes of the Sisters of our Star.

Adah. Blue represents faithfulness, as exemplified by Jephthah's Daughter, who in the springtime of her life heroically became a martyr for her convictions of right and for her father's honor. As a token of our faithful love for our sister, I deposit these flowers in her grave.

Ruth. Yellow is an emblem of fidelity, as exemplified by Ruth, who was faithful to her religion in seeking to be among people of her own belief. In memory of our sister and her faithfulness, I deposit in her grave this floral offering.

Esther. White is a symbol of purity and joy. Esther, in the purity of her devotion to her people, risked her life to save them, bringing joy to the nation. As a tribute to our departed sister, I deposit these flowers in her grave.

Martha. Green symbolizes immortality and inspires in us the hope of a life beyond the grave. As Martha evinced her splendid faith in God at the death of her brother Lazarus, so do we cling to the hope of resurrection. In token of our belief in the radiant future of our sister, I deposit in her grave this evergreen.

Electa. Red is an emblem of fervency. With religious fervor Electa befriended the needy, and endured persecution. As an assurance of our fervent friendship for our sister, I deposit in her grave this floral tribute.

W. M. These familiar lessons never lose their beauty and inspiration for us. Our sister has heard them many times, and it is proper that to her memory the old teachings should once more be pronounced. The lessons of friendship, and love, truth and fidelity, joy and hope, comfort us now in the presence of her remains.

Who can doubt that her spirit, freed, may have an opportunity to practice these teachings in a grander and fuller sense. May this hope inspire us to a greater zeal in our devotion to duty and to these high principles, so that we, too, shall be prepared to put aside this mortal body whenever the summons shall reach us, and to put on immortality.

These flowers symbolize our hope and joy in our faith in the Divine Creator. Beautiful as they are, they but faintly suggest the glories that await us in the life beyond. As an emblem of our hope in that celestial re-union, I now deposit them in the grave of our sister.

W. P. In memory of our sister, and in appreciation of her virtues, I scatter these flowers in her grave. We are reminded that as the lilies of the field are clothed in beauty, and as the birds of the air are clothed and fed, much more will our heavenly Father care for His children. Above this grave the flowers will grow, and the birds will sing in the sunshine. Let us too rejoice in the benign providence of our Father, who cares far more for us than for the birds and the flowers. He has called up the spirit of our sister. We do honor to her mortal body as the former casket of her soul, laying it away tenderly, because thus we knew her in our Chapter. When at last we are all called up before the Master, may we meet once more in fraternal love and joy. Let us pray.

PRAYER.

(By the Chaplain.)

Our Heavenly Father, look down upon us

and comfort us in our sorrow. Strengthen the loved ones of our departed sister, that they may bear her loss in meekness and in hope. Give them an added faith in Thy power, in the truth of Thy word, and in Thy blessed promises of immortality.

We thank Thee for the good example of this dear sister, who now rests from her labors. Oh teach us to number our days, that we may apply our hearts unto wisdom. May we be raised up from the death of sin unto the life of righteousness, so that, at the last, we may be found acceptable in Thy sight. So may we fall asleep peaceably in Thee, and awaken in Thy likeness, rejoicing in the goodly fellowship of those who were our loved ones here on earth. Amen.

Response. So may it be.

[A suitable hymn may be sung here, if desired, after which a benediction may be pronounced by the officiating minister, or by the Chaplain.]

MEMORIAL SERVICES.

It is the custom in many lodges to conduct annually a Memorial service in honor of the members who have departed this life during the past year. The Chapter assembles in the Chapter room, or the services may be held in a church or hall. Such ceremonies are usually open to the public.

The Altar should be draped in black. On it there should be an urn, and the regalia worn in life by the departed members in whose honor the ceremony is held. There should also be a tablet or scarf bearing the names of the departed. Flowers and candles may be used also, and a floral five-pointed star made of flowers of the appropriate colors. Music, both instrumental and vocal, is necessary in this service.

The members and officers should all wear their their badges, draped with crepe. They may march into the room in the following order, while music is played:

Marshal and Sentinel, Members, Warder and Electa, Martha and Esther, Adah and Ruth, Conductress and Associate Conductress, Secretary Treasurer, Matron and Associate Matron, Patron and Chaplain.

The Worthy Matron may preside, although she frequently asks the Worthy Patron to take her place.

The officers having taken their places, the Chapter is called up.

* * *

W. M. Friends, we are gathered here to do honor to those who have tarried with us a while, and who have been called up to their heavenly abode. Their faces are no more seen among us. Their voices are silent, yet memory persists, and we who remain unite in loving thoughts of our brothers and sisters, in songs to their memory, and in prayer. Let us sing (any suitable hymn), after which we will be led in prayer by the Chaplain.

PRAYER.

Our Father who art in heaven, in whose keeping are all Thy children in heaven and on earth, we thank Thee for thy tender providence. May we learn the lessons of this hour so that we shall cease to mourn our loved ones, and rejoice in their happy state. May we learn to hope in immortality, to trust in Thy goodness, and to labor earnestly to do Thy will.

Look down upon Thy sorrowing children

with compassion. Comfort those whose loved
ones have been taken. May they feel that
those ties of love and friendship have not
been broken, but may they realize that the
loved ones have gone to a better land, a happier home, where they await the time when all
shall be united in heavenly bliss. May our
sorrows soften our hearts, make us charitable
and kind, and turn us unto Thee.

Forgive us our sins, lend us Thy counsel
and Thy comfort, and finally unite us all in
Thy heavenly home. Amen.

[The Chapter is seated. *

Special vocal music may be introduced here.]

W. M. We are here in acknowledgement of
broken ties of tenderness and affection, of loving memories and of sincere sympathy for
friends in their bereavement. As our secretary calls the roll of our officers, may we
hear from each one with an expression of
faith and duty.

[The secretary calls the roll of officers, who
respond as follows:]

Worthy Patron. We have assembled here
to do honor to the memory of the departed,
thus performing the last sacred duties of our
Order for the Sisters and Brothers who have

gone beyond.

[If the Worthy Patron is presiding, the above response should be made by the Worthy Matron.]

Associate Matron. The messenger who summoned hence our departed friends cometh sooner or later for us all. But blessed are the dead that die in the Lord, for they rest from their labors.

Conductress. Our days are brought to an end as a tale that is told. Our stay on earth is limited and uncertain. We are constrained to serve God with constancy that we may be united later with the blessed saints in glory.

Associate Conductress. If we walk in perfect faith, we shall at length fall asleep peacefully in God, and awaken in his likeness.

Treasurer. Lay up for yourselves treasures in heaven, where neither moth nor rust doth corrupt, and where thieves do not break through nor steal: for where your treasure is, there will your heart be also.

Sentinel. But of that day and that hour no man knoweth. Watch ye, therefore, for ye know not when the master of the house cometh, at even, or at midnight or in the morning.

Warder. Take ye heed, watch and pray:

for ye know not when the time is.

Marshal. Lord Thou hast been our refuge from one generation to another. Before the mountains were brought forth, or ever the earth and the world were made, Thou art God from everlasting, and world without end.

Secretary. In that greatest of record books, the Holy Bible, we read: "This is the record, that God hath given us eternal life." In this hope we live and await the Divine summons; "Come ye blessed of my Father, inherit the Kingdom prepared for you from the foundation of the world."

[The secretary now reads the list of those members of the Chapter who have departed this life during the past year, telling about their connection with the Chapter, their official positions, and any other remarks about them, and expressions of appreciation and regret. If there are obituaries, or verses in memory of the departed, these should be read at this time.

Following the reading of the names there should be special vocal music, or any appropriate hymn may be sung by all present.

It is customary to have a special speaker to make the Memorial Address, which may be delivered at this time, the speaker being introduced by the presiding officer.

Following the Memorial Address, the Worthy Matron says:]

W. M. There yet remain to be heard the familiar lessons of our mystical Star. In times past those in whose honor we are today assembled were wont to enjoy these teachings and to profit by them. We are grateful for the good example of these companions of former days, and it is right and proper that at this time we should hear the lessons which they learned with us: the teachings which they followed so faithfully before passing on to the reward that awaits all who are found acceptable.

W. M. Sisters Adah, Ruth, Martha, and Electa, what are the lessons and tributes from the shining rays of our symbolic Star?

Adah. From the blue point of our Star, I draw this flower of blue, representing a cloudless sky. It is a symbol of faithfulness. As Jephthah's Daughter fasted and prayed in her mountain retreat, close to the cerulean blue, and remained faithful to her convictions of right and duty, so may we follow her bright example. Thus did our departed sisters and brethren, and in their memory I deposit this flower in the Memorial Urn.

Ruth. This flower of yellow I pluck from our Star, to represent the shining rays of the sun, and to symbolize constancy. Ruth por trayed in her life this virtue, as she labored in the yellow fields of Boaz, and was rewarded by the sunshine of love and friendship. In appreciation of this virtue of constancy, and of its reward, I deposit this flower in the Memorial Urn.

Esther. The white flower which I now take from our Star represents purity and joy. It teaches us that a pure life is beyond censure In memory of our departed companions who have passed into the purity and happiness o^ the life beyond, I deposit this flower in the Memorial Urn.

Martha. This green sprig which I draw from our Star. reminds us of nature's loveliness. It is an emblem of Hope and Immortality, teaching us that there is no death. The spirit continues, though the outward form may change. As Martha, beside the grave of her brother Lazarus professed her faith in immortality, I deposit this sprig of green in the Memorial Urn, signifying our hope of seeing our departed sisters and brothers in a better world.

Electa. I draw from our Star this red rose, which is a symbol of fervency. It denotes the zeal with which Electa rendered her service, a devotion which was emulated by the friends in whose memory I now deposit this rose in the Memorial Urn.

Worthy Matron. (Placing the Star on the Urn.) Sisters and Brethren, as these emblematic flowers are contained in this Urn, so the souls of our dear companions were encased in earthly bodies. The body is but an urn, an earthen jar, sealed by God while it hides His treasure, a pure soul. Now the jar is broken; the flower of the soul has gone into God's keeping.

We must know that the body is but a garment which is no longer fitting for the soul of the departed; a cage from which the soul has fled to freedom; a sea-shell out of which the pearl is gone. The shell may now be broken, but the pearl, the soul, is beyond in a place worthy of its beauty.

These, the real brothers and sisters, their spiritual selves, have passed from us for a time. When we join them we shall wonder why we wept. We shall know that where they are, there is everything to be desired: that what we now enjoy in this world is as nothing compared to the glories which are beyond. These friends whom we mourn live in unspoken bliss, and love us. They are lost to us for a time, yet in unknown happiness and amid the beauties of Paradise they live a life that has no end.

We may be sure that when we shall know, as our loved ones now know, we shall see that God is love, and that the Divine plans are all-wise. Let us then be brave and of good courage, until we too shall travel on unto our home.

The Chaplain will pronounce the benediction and dismiss us.

[* * * Calls up the Chapter.]

BENEDICTION.

The blessing of God the Father be upon us now and forever. May the tender memories of our dear friends and companions go with us on our journey through life, inspiring us to run our course in faith. May we press on toward the mark of the high calling of God, in love and service, until we shall all be united in the land where sorrow and separation are known no more forever. Amen.

Members. So may it be.

PARLIAMENTARY RULES FOR A CHAPTER OF THE ORDER OF THE EASTERN STAR.

A QUORUM.

The Charter, and the Constitutional quorum of seven members, including either the Worthy Matron, the Worthy Patron or the Associate Matron, must be present before the Chapter can be opened.

PRESIDING OFFICER.

The Worthy Matron opens the Chapter and presides. In her absence her place is filled by the Worthy Patron or the Associate Matron. The Worthy Matron may request the Worthy Patron to preside at any time.

RIGHT TO BE PRESENT.

The right of each person to be present must be ascertained before any business is transacted.

DUTIES OF THE SECRETARY.

There must be a Secretary who will call the roll, read the minutes of the last meeting, keep a record of the proceedings, and before the Chapter is closed, read the minutes of the current meeting for approval. The Secretary will also take charge of all papers and records belonging to the Chapter; receive all moneys for the Chapter; authenticate by her signature all acts, orders and proceedings. (Certain matters will also require the signature of the Worthy Matron.)

DUTIES OF THE PRESIDING OFFICER.

The Worthy Matron (or the Worthy Patron, or the Associate Matron acting for her), as presiding officer, will have the following duties:

To open the Chapter;

To announce the business and direct the proceedings;

To receive and submit properly all motions presented by members;

To put the questions to vote, and to announce the result;

To preserve order, and enforce the rules;

To receive all messages and communications and announce them to the Chapter;

To authenticate whenever necessary all acts, orders and proceedings of the Chapter by signing them;

To appoint committees, unless they are otherwise specially provided for;

To obey the commands of the Chapter, and to represent it;

To give close attention to the proceedings, and to what every member says;

The worthy Matron may read sitting, but should rise to present a motion, to put a question to the Chapter, or to conduct any of the ceremonies.

TO SECURE THE FLOOR.

When a member desires to make a statement to the Chapter, she rises in her place, and addresses the Worthy Matron, who then calls her by name. Only after receiving this recognition from the presiding officer may the member proceed to state her business. When a member has the floor she has the right to continue speaking without interruption. If, however, another member desires to say something relevant which she thinks should be heard at once, she may rise and address the chair, saying: "Worthy Matron, I rise to a point of order", (or "of privilege"). The Worthy Matron may then stop the first person from speaking, and give the second one a chance to make her statement. If the interruption is out of place it is considered disorderly.

PRECEDENCE ON THE FLOOR.

If two members rise and start to speak at the same time, the Worthy Matron recognizes the one whose voice she heard first. If there is any argument about the precedence, the Chapter may decide which one shall speak first.

TO MAKE A MOTION.

Whenever a member desires to introduce a proposition for the consideration of the Chapter she rises and after receiving recognition from the chair states the matter, and moves that it be adopted as the vote of the Chapter. Someone should then rise and second the motion, after which the Worthy Matron repeats it to the Chapter. Until the matter is stated by the presiding officer it is not a question before the Chapter. As soon as the motion is seconded however, a member can suggest changes for the mover to make in it, or that it be withdrawn. The mover has the right to change a motion or withdraw it before it has been stated by the chair. Until the motion is presented by the Worthy Matron it is not officially before the Chapter to be acted upon or considered in any manner, and no one should rise to make remarks upon it until this is done, with the exceptions mentioned above.

After the Worthy Matron has stated the question, it is before the Chapter, and the members may discuss it and debate upon it. If the motion is not worded to suit the case, or if it is considered useless, or if for any reason it is desired to postpone action on it, either definitely or indefinitely, a member may rise and make a motion to refer it to a committee, or to lay it on the table, or to propose an amendment, and the members may first vote on this proposition before voting on the first question. No new motion excepting those just mentioned, can be considered until the original motion is disposed of by vote or by the means referred to above.

A motion cannot be withdrawn after it has been made, and presented to the Chapter by the Worthy Matron (or presiding officer), except by consent of the Chapter.

AMENDMENTS

If a motion is satisfactory in its subject matter but not in its form, it may be changed by amendments. A motion to amend may be made, and this is voted on before the original question. A motion to amend the amendment is considered before the amendment, but there can be no amendment to an amendment of an amendment.

DIVIDING A QUESTION.

When a motion has several parts which could be treated separately, a member may move to divide the question into separate questions, to be presented one at a time for vote of the Chapter.

BLANKS IN A MOTION.

Sometimes a motion is introduced with blanks left for the Chapter to fill in with amounts, or times or numbers. In this case the Chapter first acts on filling out the blanks, before taking action on the motion. To do this a motion is made covering the blanks. The Chapter votes first on the longest time, or the largest number mentioned.

MOTION TO RECONSIDER.

If it is desired to vote again on a question which has previously been decided by vote, a member who voted with the majority may make a motion to reconsider the question. If the motion is carried, the subject is re-opened and may be debated and voted on as if it had never been before the Chapter.

PREVIOUS QUESTION.

A motion for the previous question cannot be considered. That is, it is not customary for the Worthy Matron to ask: "Are you ready for the question?" or, "Shall the main question now be put?"

MOTION TO ADJOURN.

A motion to adjourn cannot be considered in this order, as the regular closing ceremonies are always used.

COMMITTEES

A committee may consider only the matter referred to it, and has no legal power to do anything except the business for which it is instituted.

A committee should submit a report on which the majority of the committee agree, but a report of the minority may also be made. The chairman of a committee, or person selected to read it, presents the report.

The report of the committee need not be

accepted. It may be given to another committee, or the original committee may be commissioned to act further. It may be thus "recommitted" at any time before final action, and it is then before a committee as if for the first time.

In submitting a report, the chairman presents it, and then she, or another member, moves that it be accepted. A vote is then taken as to whether it shall be accepted.

COMMITTEE OF THE WHOLE.

It is not customary in this Order to form a committee of the whole.

PROCEDURE IN VOTING.

Petitions for the degrees or membership can only be voted upon at a regular meeting. They may be voted upon at any regular meeting.

Officers are elected annually.

The elective officers must be elected by separate and majority ballot.

The Worthy Matron directs the balloting, but the ballot-box is in charge of the Associate Conductress. She presents it first to the Worthy Matron and Worthy Patron for their inspection. After that she may present it to them for their votes, and to each member in turn for the ballot. She may, instead of doing this, place it upon the Altar after inspection, when each member goes up and deposits a ballot. There must be no crowding, but each one must remain several steps away from the Altar while the one ahead is casting a ballot.

After all of the members entitled to vote have cast their ballots the ballot is declared closed by the Worthy Matron, who directs the Associate Conductress to carry the ballot box to the West and to the East. She then takes it to the Associate Matron, who examines the ballots, and reports the result. Then she presents it to the Worthy Matron and Worthy Patron who examine the ballot, and the Worthy Matron announces the result.

FORM OF
PETITION FOR DEGREES

....192..

To the Worthy Matron, Officers and Members of
.... *Chapter, No.* ....

Order of the Eastern Star:

The undersigned respectfully petitions to receive the degrees of the Order of the Eastern Star and become a member of your Chapter. If accepted........he pledges ....self to a cheerful obedience to the laws of the Order.

Signed ....
Residence ....
.... of..............................
of........................ Lodge, No. ....
A. F. & A. M. ....

Have you ever before petitioned a Regularly Constituted Chapter of the O. E. S.? Ans....................
How long have you lived in this state?
Ans. ....
How long have you lived in the jurisdiction of this Chapter? Ans. ....
Recommended by:
....
....

Referred to the following Committee on Character:
....
....
....

REPORT

The undersigned, your Committee on Character in the case of ....,
a petitioner for the degrees, respectfully report.......
favorable to........admission thereto.
Committee on Character:
....
....
....

FORM OF
PETITION FOR AFFILIATION

.....................................192...

To the Worthy Matron, Officers and Members of
.... *Chapter, No.* ....

Order of the Eastern Star:
The undersigned, late a member of..................
.............................Chapter, No. ...... of
....
solicits affiliation with your Chapter. If this petition
be granted, ... he pledges .... self
to a careful obedience of the laws of the Order.

    Signed ....
    Residence ....

Recommended by:

    ....
    ....

Referred to the following Committee on Character:

    ....
    ....
    ....

REPORT

.............................192..

The undersigned, your Committee on Character in the
    case of ....
    a petitioner for affiliation, respectfully report........
    favorable to ....admission hereto.

Committee on Character:

    ....
    ....
    ....

A dimit from the Chapter of which the petitioner was
last a member should accompany this petition.

FORM OF DIMIT

To the Membership of the Order of the Eastern Star:

This dimit bears witness that................ .... was received into .... Chapter, No. ......, of .... in 19... And that having paid all dues and being free from all charges, ... he is at .... own request lawfully dismissed from membership therein.

Attested by my hand and the Seal of the Chapter, this .... day of ...., 19...

....

Secretary.